America's
Worship Wars

America's
Worship Wars

Terry W. York

HENDRICKSON
PUBLISHERS

© 2003 by Terry W. York

Hendrickson Publishers, Inc.
P. O. Box 3473
Peabody, Massachusetts 01961-3473

Printed in the United States of America

Second Printing—November 2003

Library of Congress Cataloging-in-Publication Data

York, Terry W.
    America's worship wars / Terry W. York.
      p. cm.
    Includes bibliographical references and index.
    ISBN 1-56563-490-X (pbk. : alk. paper)
    1. Public worship—History—20th century. 2. United States—Church history—20th century. I. Title.
    BV8.Y67 2003
    264'.00973'090511—dc21

                                  2003011106

It is acknowledged from the outset that worship "wars" are not combat. The use of the term in this book is in no way meant to demean the traumatic experiences of those who have served in combat. Their suffering and sacrifice must never be taken lightly. This book is dedicated to those whose sacrifices in real wars have made possible the luxury of our worship wars. I wish to give special recognition to one of that group, my father, Sergeant Major Maurice W. York, United States Marine Corps, Retired: from the islands of the South Pacific through the jungles of South Vietnam . . . *Semper Fidelis*. This Baptist deacon and Sunday School teacher has taught me more than he realizes about war, peace, and life.

Terry W. York

Table of Contents

Introduction

'Mid toil and tribulation,
and tumult of her war,
she waits the consummation
of peace forever more;
till with the vision glorious,
her longing eyes are blest,
and the great church victorious
shall be the church at rest.

Samuel J. Stone[1]

What you are about to read could be thought of as a memoir. It is a mixture of documented history, observation, and interpretation. Like any wartime memoir, it is one person's intense, but limited commentary. Its documented history is true and its observation and interpretation are faithfully recounted and presented. It is a large war observed from a small perch. In the case of this book, the author's small perches were as a high school student, a young Marine, a minister of music and youth in small to medium-sized Baptist churches, a denominational employee, an associate pastor of a large Baptist church, and a seminary/university professor. I saw a great deal, but not all, and what I did see was through the several lenses just mentioned and their accompanying prejudices. This is not an apology. It is an invitation to dialogue. What did you see? What do you see? How would you interpret it? What can our interpretations contribute to the future?

The theo-political "wars" experienced inside the confines of some of America's major Christian denominations are but subsets

---

[1] "The Church's One Foundation," in *Lyra Fidelium: Twelve Hymns of the Twelve Articles of the Apostle's Creed* (London: Parker, 1866).

of the nation's larger "culture wars."[2] Since the early 1960s Americans have become sadly accustomed to using the word "war" in a colloquial way. Even so, it seems an awkward juxtaposition to include the words "worship" and "wars" in the same sentence or title. Yet, strangely, the two events have something in common. Both worship and war engage the extreme depth of the human soul, even though they are poles apart in human behavior. Both call forth risk, confrontation, and sacrifice. The title of this book is intended to describe a situation in which gains were made against determined opposition and treasured values were defended, sometimes at great cost. In researching the dynamics and the discourse of change that took place in worship in the United States during the last four decades of the twentieth century, one often encounters words such as war, battle, kill, camps, tribes, strategies, bastion, conflict, camouflage, advance, retreat, surrender, fronts, lasting peace, truce, revolution, battlefield, and casualties. These words are from the vocabulary of war. It is disturbing that commentators, theologians, and worship leaders found these words and phrases to be the most descriptive.

Granted, the Apostle Paul used the vocabulary of warfare when he encouraged the Ephesians to "put on the full armor of God," but that was so they could "stand against the wiles of the devil" (Eph 6:11, NRSV). The struggle in question was "against the rulers, against the authorities, against the cosmic powers of this present darkness, against the spiritual forces of evil in the heavenly places" (v. 12, NRSV). Their armament was not for struggle against brothers and sisters in the community of Christ-followers, fellow worshipers. It appears, then, that America's worship wars were (and are) civil wars, wars between citizens of the same homeland. I speak not of their American homeland, but of their citizenship in the kingdom of God.

The term "worship wars" began to surface in the mid-1990s in the writings of theologians such as Ted Peters of Pacific Lutheran Theological Seminary and the Graduate Theological Union of Berkeley, California, and ministry practitioners such as Marva J. Dawn of Christians Equipped for Ministry in Vancouver, Washington. Ted Peters, in an article titled "Worship Wars"[3] suggested that

---

[2] For an excellent understanding of this concept read James Davison Hunter, *Culture Wars: The Struggle to Define America* (New York: Basic Books, 1991).

[3] Ted Peters, "Worship Wars," *Dialog* 33.3 (Summer 1994): 166.

worship wars parallel culture wars, and that culture wars are inevitable in a social environment of pluralism. Using militaristic language, he put forth three possible strategies for the Christian faith: advance, retreat, and "swallow the Trojan horse."

The advance strategy is to proclaim the truth of the Christian gospel as universally valid for all people of all times and places, and to present this proclamation both inside the churches and in the public square. The retreat strategy would be to create an ecclesiology that separates the church from the public arena. The Trojan horse strategy would be to turn the church itself into a naked public square, to ape the surrounding culture by giving up any sense of center and swallowing pluralism whole (p. 166). Examples of each strategy are easily found.

In her salient book *Reaching Out without Dumbing Down*, Marva J. Dawn laments the "bitter battles" of the church's "worship wars" and asks if we can "find common criteria by which to assess what we are doing in worship so that we can bring together opposing sides of various arguments, so that we can truly be the Church as we talk together about our worship practices."[4]

Our God, the only true and living God, is quite clear on the matter: we are to have no other gods (Exodus 20:1–8). Yet, we have a tendency to be blinded to the existence of potential "other gods."

Consider, for example, the fact that Americans love efficiency. Americans love to get the most productivity they can out of any dollar or hour they invest. It's a matter of resources and economy. We like to be smart when it comes to using our time wisely. We love, whenever possible, to kill two birds with one stone . . . one bird per stone is not as efficient, not as productive, not as smart.

Americans also love comfort. A great deal of time and effort is invested in making our lives more comfortable and generally, "easier." We send food back at the restaurant if it is not exactly as we ordered it. We take cushions to sporting events, even the symphony. We look forward to weekends, vacations, and retirement. Rest is biblical. Yet, while Jesus' yoke may be easy and his burden light, comfort is not always what is promised or prophesied. But Americans love comfort. We want to be comfortable when we walk, travel, shop, go home, go to work, even when we go to church.

How do these thoughts about efficiency and comfort contribute to worship wars? Let's explore the possibilities. The word

---

[4] Marva J. Dawn, *Reaching Out without Dumbing Down* (Grand Rapids, Mich.: Eerdmans, 1995), 3.

"worship" is used somewhat sparingly and carefully, even in our casual and ever-expanding vocabulary. It isn't used, for instance, quite as much as the word "love" or even "adore." Perhaps that's because it is commonly accepted that worship identifies who or what our god is. Consider again, the first commandment.

> "Then God spoke all these words: I am the Lord your God, who brought you out of the land of Egypt, out of the house of slavery: you shall have no other gods before me." (NRSV)

A number of writers including names such as Walter Brueg-gemann and Marva Dawn[5] have alerted us to the fact that in our worship there are some very noble, "little g" gods that can easily and subtly climb up on the throne and sit next to the only "big G" God. These "gods" often relate to our desire to not be discomforted in worship and/or our desire to accomplish other noble things while we are worshiping. We don't want to worship other gods, but sometimes we invite them into the throne room and up onto the throne unwittingly, often with the best of intentions.

How can we identify the "little g" gods and keep them off of the throne? I think there is a simple screening process. I refer to it as the *"worship and"* test. If we are to worship the one true God *and* no others, the "and" will identify any other contenders for the throne.

What are *some* of the contenders? Allow me to dare a *few* suggestions. One is patriotism. When, in a worship service, we worship *and* declare our patriotism, we have allowed a noble "little 'g' god" to join the one true God on the throne. I am a former Marine and come from a family of Marines. I consider myself to be a patriotic person. But patriotism must not be worshiped nor seen as a form of worship.

When we make adjustments that allow us to worship God *and* advance the cause of church growth we have allowed a little "g" god to share the throne. When we declare that our service is designed to worship *and* evangelize, we have allowed a noble little "g" god to share the throne.

Is such a statement anti-church growth? Absolutely not. Is it anti-evangelism? Absolutely not. But, corporately, for one hour a week, at least, we need to disown the god of efficiency and worship the God of our salvation. Worship unifies. Agendas divide.

---

[5] See Walter Brueggemann, *Israel's Praise: Doxology against Idolatry and Ideology* (Philadelphia: Fortress, 1988) and Dawn, *Reaching Out without Dumbing Down.*

"Worship *and"* presupposes and identifies an agenda. People will "go to war" over intense and deeply held agendas.

Then what shall we preach if not evangelism, if not church growth, if not the occasional patriotic sermon? Isn't almost every likely sermon topic an "and"?

The Christian worship experience has long been divided into two sections: the service of the Word and the service of the Table. The service of the Word has been, since the beginning of Christian worship, the recounting of the life and works of Jesus and the reading and interpreting of Scripture; what some would call the preaching part of the service. The service of the Table has been the Eucharist or observance of the Lords Supper. Today, even in free-church congregations that don't celebrate the meal each Sunday, the distinction is observed, allowing expressions of thanksgiving to substitute for the Lord's Supper. They may be mingled in bits and pieces rather than neatly gathered into two distinct and separate sections, but service of the Word and service of the Table are present.

This brings us to the balance for the "worship and" concept. The balance is this, as human beings, we are confined and affected by time and space, or, if you will, time and place. We want to offer God unadulterated, pure worship, but as humans we are unable to do so. When we enter the place of worship at the given time of worship, we bring with us all of who we are; what we have been doing, what has been done to us, our failures and successes, our tears of sorrow and of joy, our likes and dislikes. We may dress up, but the clean clothes and clean faces only mask life's bruises.

While admonishing us to avoid the extremes of "the traditional Protestant 'preaching service'" and "mass recited in the absence of a congregation, or celebrated in a language not familiar to the people," William Stringfellow wrote of the liturgy:

> *This* is the time and *this* is the place and *this* is the way, in a most immediate sense, in which the whole, manifold, existential involvement of the members of Christ's Body in the everyday life of the world—both all that seems good and which men are tempted to honor or praise, and all that seems evil and which men are fond of rationalizing or denying—is offered and consecrated for the discretion of Christ Himself, the Redeemer of all men and all things [6]

---

[6] William Stringfellow, *Dissenter in a Great Society: A Christian View of America in Crisis* (New York: Holt, Rinehart and Winston, 1966), 152–53.

Preaching helps us look at and deal with our humanness in the light and perspective of Scripture. In the preaching event, worshipers are gathered into community where we can be strengthened, healed, and encouraged. Preaching, a part of the service of the Word, gathers Christ-followers back into community and gives us a Scripture-informed place to stand in order to worship. It acknowledges our struggles and hopes. As human beings we must have this kind of honest place to stand in order to offer our worship.

According to Exodus 20, however, in all of earth, even in all of heaven, there is no godly thing, no godly person, no godly cause that is worthy of worship, only God. Let's acknowledge that and practice that for at least one hour a week.

"No other gods" is an important commandment. Add-on agendas are divisive, they are "other gods." They drag worship into war. The chapters in Part II represent selected, significant "worship and . . . add-on agendas" or arenas in which such agendas exist.

Dawn, like Peters, looks to the study of culture as a means of understanding the dynamics of change in worship practice and theology. We should not be surprised at tension between culture and worship. We need only re-read the story of Cain and Abel to be reminded of the long history of the struggle. J. D. Crichton reminds us that "Worship . . . can be seen as at once reaching out to the transcendent and as embedded in human life."[7] Were worship not embedded in human life, it would not be authentic—we would not be worshiping in truth. The embeddedness is risky, however, the risk of stepping over the line between cultural relevance and cultural assimilation. During the historical period that is the focus of this study, that line became the "front."

Some feared that the line in the sand had actually been drawn in ever-hardening cement. In his article, "How Much Uniformity Can We Stand? Church and Worship in the Next Millenium," Peter C. Phan, Professor of Religion and Culture at the Catholic University of America in Washington, D.C., observed, "Both conservatives and liberals are sincerely convinced that they are the last bastion in the cosmic battle for the survival of the church." "Often," he wrote, "it is impossible to distinguish the strategies and tactics of conservatives and liberals from each other."[8]

---

[7] J. D. Crichton in *The Study of Liturgy* (eds. Cheslyn Jones et al.; rev. ed.; New York: Oxford University Press, 1992), 8.

[8] Peter C. Phan, "How Much Uniformity Can We Stand? Church and Worship in the Next Millenium," *Worship* (May 1998): 203–4.

Many churches were and, at the time of this writing, are indeed, "a gathering of various tribes with different tastes and ideas and feelings about worship."[9] One specific example can be seen in the following church newsletter column of pastor Julie Pennington-Russell:

> A number of you have been talking to me about worship at Calvary these days. This makes me very glad, because worship is something I care deeply about. What has me scratching my head lately is the variety of observations I have heard. During the past two weeks alone I have heard the following comments:
>
> - "I like the new hymns we've been singing."
> - "We're singing too many songs that nobody knows. Give me Fanny Crosby."
> - "I have had a real sense of God's presence lately."
> - "Worship feels cold and formal to me—too liturgical."
> - "Calvary is too casual—too touchy, feely. What's with all these choruses?"
> - "When are we going to start singing more choruses?"
> - "I love the sense of reverence we have in worship, especially the times of silence before prayer."
> - "The spaces of silence in worship make me bored and uncomfortable."
> - "I'd like to hear more classical music in worship."
> - "Do you think we could buy a set of drums?"
>
> You get the picture. I kid you not; all of the above comments come from people who call Calvary home—people who are invested in the life and ministry of this church.[10]

The situation just described could be seen as nothing more than the typical differences of opinion within a specific congregation. That isn't new. But, in the environment of worship wars, one becomes somewhat "gun-shy." Trust and open dialogue become endangered by suspicion. Steve Bierly, pastor of the Cobblestone Church in Schenectady, New York, also saw the line and perceived it to be hardening when he wrote,

> The music-style-in-worship debate is nothing if not divisive. Those who prefer traditional hymns clash with those bringing drums and

---

[9] Carol Doran and Thomas H. Troeger, *Trouble at the Table: Gathering Tribes for Worship* (Nashville: Abingdon, 1992), 12.

[10] Julie Pennington-Russell, "From Your Pastor," in *The Tower,* weekly newsletter of Calvary Baptist Church, Waco, Texas; November 4, 1998.

guitars into the sanctuary. People on each side of the debate believe
they are defenders of the way God wants to be worshiped.[11]

What happened, and when? Some practitioners and scholars
might begin a study such as this in the decade of the 1950s. In
1956, Geoffrey Beaumont led the Twentieth Century Church Light
Music Group to publish the *Twentieth-Century Folk Mass*. Known
as the "Jazz Mass," this adventure in church music had a noticeable
effect on the 1962 British publication *The Baptist Hymn Book*. Even
though a limited number of Catholic hymns had been at home in
Protestant hymnals for some time, this particular instance of influence was something more than ecumenical. This was jazz. This
was the music of *Broadway*, not "the narrow way." Careful ecume-
nism was one thing. Blatant invasion by the secular was quite
another.

Still, such convergence was seen as exploratory. Even with the
blessing of being included in a hymnal, the jazz influence was considered isolated experimentation. If, however, this incident was
nothing more than a benign blessing, a formal "baptism" was about
to happen. In 1962, the Second Vatican Council convened in Rome.

Not surprisingly, the significance of the decrees of Vatican II
has met with differing interpretations. Matthew Fox wrote, "For
Catholicism, Vatican II marked a turning point in its spirituality as
the 'world' was acknowledged as a rightful place to encounter
God. Thus was continued the struggles with the postmedieval
world initiated by the Reformation."[12] Yet others would argue that
Catholicism is historically incarnational in its theology and piety,
deeply rooted in the world as the rightful place to encounter God.
This relationship is evident in the Middle Ages, but also in the
baroque period as evident in art, architecture, music, etc. Vatican II
did not mark a turn to the world in this sense. Vatican II certainly
intended to mark a path for the Catholic Church according to the
"signs of the times" of the world of today, but here the term
"world" does not mean the created realm but what we would now
call the "modern," "post-modern," or "post-Christian" world. Vatican II had no special interest in the relation of Church to world,
but in the encounter of Church to the secularized world.[13]

---

[11] Steve Bierly, "Sparring Over Worship," *Leadership* (Winter 1997): 37.

[12] Matthew Fox, *On Becoming a Musical, Mystical Bear* (New York:
Paulist, 1976), 9.

[13] Father Timothy Vaverek, St. Joseph Catholic Church, Waco, Texas,
in an e-mail to the author, March 25, 2002.

Some were convinced that the Catholic Church had been marched to the brink of the slippery slope. Avery Dulles reported, "After the Council [Vatican II] . . . some priests seemed to be imitating popular entertainers and talkshow hosts to the detriment of the solemnity and formality that by right pertained to the liturgy."[14] The impact of Vatican II is attested by the fact that debate over its findings continues decades later. "Thirty years ago this December, the Second Vatican Council came to an end. Did the publication of its decrees signify the completion of the renewal of the church that the council represented, or did those documents mark only the beginning of a process that has not yet been completed? This question is still being debated."[15]

The openness, the changes, and the resistance were not isolated to Rome or even the Catholic Church. Vatican II "was a gathering that not only had profound impact on the Catholic Church, but also had an influence on many other churches and religions, and on the world as a whole."[16]

In the United States, a surprising religious phenomenon was emerging as the cultural upheaval of the 1960s was waning. Not only was the culture forcing its way into the church, unwilling to wait for the historical pace of assimilation, the gospel was beginning to march in the street, unwilling to be boxed in by tradition. ". . . When I entered the University of California [Berkeley] I met the 'Jesus Movement,' a spiritual counterpart to the 1960s counterculture. I followed them to Calvary Chapel in Costa Mesa, California, and witnessed something no Lutheran boy could imagine. It was a world of rock 'n' roll healing services in Hawaiian shirts, leather Bibles, and speaking in tongues in the thousands."[17] In 1971, major magazines and television networks in the United States were naming, reporting, and thus legitimizing the Jesus Movement in a way that only the media can. The relationship of church and culture was being redefined, perhaps undefined. The potential for good in the spread and application of the gospel was enormous. So, too, the potential for conflict and conformity.

---

[14] Avery Dulles, "The Ways We Worship," *First Things* (March 1998): 28.

[15] Thomas P. Rausch, S.J., "The Unfinished Agenda of Vatican II," *America* (June 17, 1995): 23–27.

[16] Brennen R. Hill, *Exploring Catholic Theology: God, Jesus, Church, and Sacraments* (Mystic, Conn.: Twenty-Third Publications, 1995), 222.

[17] Gary M. Burge, "Missing God at Church?" *Christianity Today* (October 6, 1997): 22.

A community's theology and worship cannot be divorced. Therefore, practical or applied theology (gospel in the street) fueled the concept of practical or applied worship (culture in the sanctuary). "War," a term all too common in the culture, seemed destined to become equally as common in the church. Virtually every denomination attached this new worship streamer to its battle flag.

Because of the chronological parameters of this book (Vatican II to the twenty-first century), the past tense *(veterans,* not *soldiers)* is used in the narrative. The truth is that at the time of the writing of this book, the worship wars continue. And now, this bit of wartime advice: "Keep your head down" . . . not to take cover, but in prayer.

Part I

THE WINDS OF WAR

ONE

The 1960s: A Time of Change

Change in the basic structure and norms of American society surfaced too suddenly for any kind of orderly response. "Surfaced" seems to be the appropriate word because no cultural "sea-change" of this magnitude can be said to have been instantaneous, not even the spark that set it in motion. Charles A. Reich, in *The Greening of America,* suggests that the building pressure could be attributed to "the promise of life that [was] made to young Americans by all of our affluence, technology, liberation, and ideals, and the threat to that promise posed by everything from neon ugliness and boring jobs to the Vietnam War and the shadow of nuclear holocaust."[1]

Was there an igniting spark for the culture wars? If so, a number of events are candidates for the dubious honor. The radical social disorder and re-ordering of the 1960s was stunningly deep and foundational. The established society, frozen by shock, turned from watching the spectacle on TV only long enough to fight back in fits of defensive reaction and rhetoric. Fear and anger slowed the emergence of thoughtful dialogue and positive initiatives. Fires consumed the inner city, American flags, bras, crosses and draft-cards. The United States "dodged the bullet" of the Cuban missile crisis only to find itself looking down rifle barrels of the Viet Cong overseas and assassins at home. The hippies, with their guitars, were caroling their message of peace and love at the door of the national capital and the local sanctuary. King David's advocacy of stringed instruments notwithstanding, the church saw the guitars of "Peter, Paul, and Mary" as swords of change, not plowshares of peace. The drums (and hair) of Ringo Starr and all others like him and his group were heard by the established society as the threatening drums of a war dance. The drums were getting louder, not

---

[1] Charles A. Reich, *The Greening of America* (New York: Random House, 1970), 218.

softer. The symbolism was too striking. Guitars and drums and all they represented were to be kept out of the Anglo, main-line churches. Songs and sermons of peace were to be of peace through victory; victory in our streets, in Southeast Asia, and in our sanctuaries. This, to counter the speeches and music of anti-war and anti-establishment protestors whose visions of victory were threatening to all that *privileged* Americans held dear. The determined established church shut its doors and windows to the outside world (mirroring the captivity of Americans in North Vietnam), aging its songs and gagging its message. Embracing Christ-like responses to poverty, racism, and violence seemed beyond the reach of a church whose arms were frozen in defense. Issues of peace and justice were not foreign to the church, but the physical appearance, tactics, and pace demanded by the advocates of change were.

The church had not thought this deeply, had not entertained the prospect of such radical involvement, had not considered such radical change for centuries. The issues were being forced. Defensiveness, even if just to buy some time for contemplation, was a common reaction. But, there were cracks in the defenses. One of the cracks was the Second Vatican Council.

Vatican II

Convened by Pope John XXIII on October 11, 1962, the Second Vatican Council met in Rome in four sessions. Session I ended on December 8, 1962. Session II was from September 29 to December 4, 1963. Between the first two sessions of the Vatican Council, Pope John XXIII died (June 3, 1963) and Pope Paul VI assumed leadership of the Church (June 21). The more than 2000 bishops met for Session III from September 14 to November 21, 1964. The final session was from September 14 to December 8, 1965. Meeting between these four plenary sessions, a number of conciliar commissions diligently worked on various specific assignments.

The first two documents to come from the work of the conciliar commissions were made public on December 4, 1963. They were the "Constitution on the Sacred Liturgy" and the "Decree on the Instruments of Social Communication" (or "Decree on the Mass Media"). One cannot escape the implications of these particular documents being released first and simultaneously. Here we have fresh statements of renewal concerning the

Roman Church's focus on God (worship) and focus on the world (mass media).

Without going deeply—but going deeply enough to have a working understanding of Catholic liturgical theology—for Roman Catholics the Eucharistic liturgy, or the "mass," sacramentally makes present the saving work of Christ's death and resurrection. For this reason, Vatican II reaffirms that the reality encountered at mass (i.e., Christ's Passover) is the source and summit of Christian life, worship, and evangelism. In such a theology, to make Christian worship accessible to humanity is an essential part of fully proclaiming the gospel of salvation and of bringing humanity to new life in Christ. However, in an evangelical setting (Protestant churches that believe in salvation by faith in Jesus alone, without additional reliance on the sacraments), the Lord's Supper is most often referred to as an ordinance, not a sacrament. Further, the observance of the Lord's Supper or communion is not uniformly nor often centrally experienced in Protestant worship. In Catholic and Protestant settings, then, weaving together the reform of worship and communication to the world (human beings) moves toward two similar but separate ends. In one setting (Catholic), such relatedness or convergence enhances the work of worship/salvation. In the other (Protestant), it serves to blur the lines of definition between worship and salvation. In evangelical settings when salvation and worship are seen as overlapping circles, it is quite easy for the lines of definition between worship and evangelism to be the next to become blurred. In fact that is what happened in the worship theology of many Protestant congregations and denominations. Such overlap can call the proponents of any one circle to "take up arms" in defense against the undue influence of the others.

Certainly, the influence of evangelistic fervor had been evident in the worship practices of many American evangelical churches long before Vatican II. It was known as "revivalism." However, the Council's work seemed to create a general atmosphere (to the extent that particular evangelicals were aware of the pronouncements) in which such blurring of worship and evangelism seemed to be validated as efficiency. Yet, it can be argued that outreach was not the goal of Vatican II in its liturgical reform, that the purpose of liturgy, and hence the reason for liturgical reform, was the full, active, and conscious participation of Christians in the life of Christ.

Consider the following statements from "The Constitution on the Sacred Liturgy." I will use italics for emphasis. In the "Introduction," paragraph 1, the purpose of the Vatican Council is stated: "The sacred council has set out . . . to strengthen whatever serves to call *all of humanity* into the *church's* fold."[2] A few pages later, in the section titled "III. The Reform of the Sacred Liturgy," paragraph 21, we read that, "It is the wish of the church to undertake a *careful* general reform of the liturgy in order that the *Christian* people may be more certain to derive an abundance of graces from it."[3]

To be fair, there is no indication that the simultaneous desires just cited to "call all of humanity into the church's fold" and "undertake a careful general reform of the liturgy in order that the Christian people may be more certain to derive an abundance of graces from it" were meant to influence each other. Indeed, a clearer understanding could be that the issue of the post-conciliar Catholic Church is not between the worship and the evangelistic functions of liturgy. Rather, the issues have been the twin struggles of how to adapt the liturgy to Christians in various cultures and how to adapt the preaching of the gospel to various cultures. An attempt on the part of the Council to offer some preventative guidance on these very issues seems evident in the sentence, "The competent territorial ecclesiastical authority . . . must, in this matter, carefully and prudently consider which elements from the traditions and cultures of individual peoples might appropriately be admitted into divine worship."[4] Given the revivalistic bent of many of America's free-church denominations and congregations, an unofficial, ill-informed, and casual observation of Roman Catholicism's move toward relevance could validate their own combining of worship and evangelism and energize their efforts to mirror the surrounding culture. Translated into evangelical Protestant terminology, "competent ecclesiastical authority" could refer to those in higher education, denominational judicatories, pastors, ministers of music, deacons, or a majority vote of the members in the pews. In the "free-church," who gets to decide? Here are the makings of a war.

---

[2] Austin Flannery, O.P., ed., *Vatican Council II: The Basic Sixteen Documents: Constitutions, Decrees, Declarations* (Northport, N.Y.: Costello Publishing Company, 1996), 117.

[3] Ibid., 126.

[4] Ibid., 132.

Specific statements within Vatican II's "Decree on the Mass Media" can be seen now as arenas for significant disagreement among Christian worshipers (first Catholic, then Protestant) as technology advanced throughout the remainder of the twentieth century. The conciliar commission that prepared "The Constitution on the Sacred Liturgy" seemed to send a message to their counterparts who were, at the same time, preparing the "Decree on the Mass Media." Paragraph 20 of the Sacred Liturgy document states that the "Transmission of the sacred rites by radio and television, especially the Mass, should be done with delicacy and dignity."[5] It is interesting to compare this statement with a portion of Paragraph 14 from the "Decree on the Mass Media." There we read, "Ample encouragement should be given to Catholic transmissions which invite listeners and viewers to share in the life of the church . . . their transmissions should be marked by high quality and effectiveness."[6]

These two statements need not have trouble co-existing within the desires and intent of any Christian broadcasters, especially for members of the same tradition or congregation. The statements are complementary, and even mutually enhancing. High quality and effectiveness are entirely appropriate goals for any radio or television production. The decree is simply admonishing those stations that broadcast and telecast the sacred rites to do so with delicacy and dignity. "The 'effectiveness' of the liturgy," wrote Father Timothy Vaverek, "is by the power of the Holy Spirit and in accord with the disposition of those participating (all of whom are baptized Christians)—hence liturgical reform and media broadcasts should be designed in a dignified and delicate manner that allows Christians to enter in to the celebration."[7] But he admitted that "there may even be Catholics" who wish the liturgy to be an effective marketing tool as well as those who see it primarily as worship. The intent of the Vatican II decrees notwithstanding, in what ways and by what measurement could or should a worship service, broadcast or not, be deemed "effective"? When might the technical demands of radio or television production impinge on the content of the broadcast or telecast? What might a radio or television producer do to

---

[5] Ibid., 126.
[6] Ibid., 546.
[7] Let me take this opportunity to thank Father Timothy for reading this chapter and making helpful suggestions.

insure or enhance effectiveness? All this will be explored more thoroughly in chapter seven.

The "Decree on the Mass Media" recognized that "the genius of humankind, especially in our times, has produced marvelous technical inventions from creation, with God's help. . . . Chief among them are . . . radio, television and others of like nature. . . . But the church also knows that they can be used in ways which are damaging and contrary to the Creator's design."[8] Advances in technology and its accessibility, as well as differing ideas about the place and definition of "effectiveness," increasingly affected the worship of local congregations during the closing decades of the twentieth century.

Even though the decrees of Vatican II had authority only over the Roman Catholic Church, the reforms, fleshed out in the local parishes, had an influence on neighboring Protestant congregations and their denominational judicatories. Notice this report from a 1962 publication:

> Protestant opinion about Catholics, or for that matter, Catholic opinion about Protestants is very different if you take those under thirty-five or forty years of age than if you take those over forty . . . The most interesting thing that was discovered was probably the marked cleavage in opinion between Protestants under thirty-five and those over. The latter, the older generation, were deeply disturbed . . . The tendency of these varying attitudes is obvious: older-generation attitudes make for the exacerbation of religious tensions; younger-generation attitudes make for their mitigation.[9]

The pressure to change moved "up and down" denominational structures with varying mixtures of enthusiasm and hesitancy. Matters were not improved when the openness to dialogue between Catholics and Protestants was more enthusiastically present among the young than among the older members. Whether Catholic or Protestant, denomination or congregation, those in authority can find their efforts toward reform of the traditional stretched toward rejection of the traditional. Therefore, something as beautiful as ecumenical efforts (one area of change) toward worship reform (a second area of change) was vulnerable to determined advocacy and resistance.

---

[8] Flannery, 539.
[9] Will Herberg, "Protestant-Catholic Tensions in Pluralistic America," in *Cities and Churches: Readings on the Urban Church* (ed. Robert Lee; Philadelphia: Westminster, 1962), 291–92.

Anti-Establishment

"Anti-Establishment" is a term often applied to the over-arching social environment of the 1960s. It was a "movement" that was often outshined by its more luminary subsets. Norman F. Cantor helps us to "unpack" the larger movement:

> The young were challenging the middle-aged on moral grounds. Their important and continuing quarrel with American life could burst out anywhere: on college campuses, in the ghettoes, even in the squarest suburbs. The young simply refused to accept the values and institutions of their parents and teachers. Such a refusal was at the root . . . of political, social and aesthetic movements as yet unrecognized.[10]

Discontent of the young with the old did not begin in the 1960s. But for this generation it was more than a testing of young wings. This was a fundamental questioning of institutions that had existed long enough to no longer be seen as institutions by their adherents. This was an eroding of traditions, a questioning of values, far more than just chafing under the rules. Expressing their viewpoint, the young would not allow the institution of patriotism or industrial vitality to hide the deep-seated wrongs of the Vietnam War, even though their protests were often labeled "riots" by the "establishment." They would not allow free enterprise to hide the injustice of poverty. They would not allow social order and orderliness to hide suffocating racism. They would not allow economic expansion to hide ecological threats to the environment. They would not let the threat of responsive nuclear annihilation hide true peace. Once the movement was underway it could not be contained. The questioning attacked the moorings of authority, responsibility, marriage, and sexuality.

Claiming that this atmosphere of dissent had its roots in lesser-known movements of the 1950s, Theodore Roszak wrote in 1968:

> The fact is, it is the young who have in their own amateurish, even grotesque way, gotten dissent off the adult drawing board. They have torn it out of the books and journals an older generation of radicals authored, and they have fashioned it into a style of life. They have turned the hypotheses of disgruntled elders into experiments, though

---

[10]Norman F. Cantor, *The Age of Protest: Dissent and Rebellion in the Twentieth Century* (New York: Hawthorn Books, 1969), 306–7.

often without the willingness to admit that one may have to concede failure at the end of any true experiment.[11]

Rosazk had reservations about what he was observing. What he saw, we now look back and see as potential battle lines:

> When all is said and done, however, one cannot help being ambivalent toward this compensatory dynamism of the young. For it is, at last, symptomatic of a thoroughly diseased state of affairs. It is not ideal, it is probably not even good that the young should bear so great a responsibility for inventing or initiating for their society as a whole. It is too big a job for them to do successfully. It is indeed tragic that in a crisis that demands the tact and wisdom of maturity, everything that looks most hopeful in our culture should be building from scratch—as must be the case when the builders are absolute beginners.[12]

These "beginners" felt they were "building from scratch" because of all that was seemingly crumbling around them. They had lived their entire lives under the threat of nuclear war. They had seen, via television, the assassinations of President Kennedy, Martin Luther King Jr., and Robert Kennedy. These beginners watched each evening as Walter Cronkite showed them the horrors of combat; combat being waged by young men their age. American cities were going up in smoke. The establishment was not only being questioned, it was being escaped from through drug abuse, it was being rejected, burned, and shot.

As noted earlier, the younger generation was fashioning their anti-establishment protests into a lifestyle. Perhaps the most notable newly fashioned lifestyle was that of the "hippies." Their goal seemed not so much to move society through a process of change as it was to model the end result of such change. The message of these "flower children" was peace and love. Both peace and love seemed to them to be obviously and sufficiently "anti" to the "establishment's" way of doing business. But peace and love are the message of the church. Should not the peace and love (to say nothing of justice) agenda of the "flower children" have been seen by the followers of the Rose of Sharon and the Lily of the Valley as invitations to join the movement, to fly their Kingdom of

---

[11] Theodore Roszak, *The Making of a Counter Culture: Reflections on the Technocratic Society and Its Youthful Opposition* (Garden City, N.Y.: Doubleday, 1968), 26.

[12] Ibid.

God flag against the winds of the kingdom of the world? For many white, Anglo-Saxon, Protestant congregations, both the American flag and the Christian flag hung limp from their stands in the sanctuary. Yet, if one were to watch closely, they might have seen the slightest flutter. The winds of war . . . worship wars, were beginning to blow.

Robert W. Shaffer, then Minister of Word and Sacraments of the First Presbyterian Church of Glassboro, New Jersey, wrote in 1967:

> The living Christ is always calling for new wineskins which contain but do not stop the fermentation. Each wineskin has its limit of stretching; the ever-new wine does not . . . we were more able to see the relationship between what matters most and the world in which we live, including our occupations, leisure time, and active commitments to civil rights, urban renewal, the war on poverty, the county hospital needs, and so on.[13]

> "As culture changes, so the way Christian worship in that culture will change. The gospel must always address a world in rebellion against God."[14]

---

[13] Robert W. Shaffer, "Fractured Forms," in *The Church Creative: A Reader on the Renewal of the Church* (ed. M. Edward Clark et al.; Nashville: Abingdon, 1967), 93.

[14] Harry L. Poe, "Worship and Ministry," in *New Dimensions in Evangelical Thought* (ed. David S. Dockery; Downers Grove, Ill.: InterVarsity, 1998).

TWO

Denominational Boundaries Breaking Down

> *When we have no agreements about why we belong together, the institutions we create to serve us become battlegrounds that serve no one.*
>
> Margaret J. Wheatley and Myron Kellner-Rogers[1]

When the United States of America was born, many of the denominations within its borders "were, by virtue of their relationship to churches in Europe, developed by the parish system."[2] This concept of a local congregation being comprised of all the churchgoers in a given neighborhood continued well into the mid-nineteenth century. However, about that time, "American Protestantism went over to the concept of a 'gathered community' and the parish idea was almost entirely abandoned. In many places churches of the same denomination were built around the corner from each other serving not an area but a constituency without relationship to any area."[3] This created a need for each congregation to communicate or advertise, perhaps even create, its distinctive emphases or strengths. Eventually, this included specific worship practices. Such geographic co-existence was, for the most part, cordial. Indeed, the members of the several congregations were neighbors and co-workers Monday through Saturday. But, to paraphrase Robert Frost's often quoted and mis-quoted line, "ecclesiastical fences made good neighbors."

---

[1] "The Paradox and Promise of Community," in *The Community of the Future* (ed. Frances Hesselbein et al.; San Francisco: Jossey-Bass, 1998), 17.

[2] Robert Lee, ed., *Cities and Churches: Readings on the Urban Church* (Philadelphia: Westminster, 1962), 332.

[3] Ibid.

The last three decades of the twentieth century saw a progression of cross-denominational and non-denominational activity that, building on earlier dialogue among the young, began to ignore some of those fences. Indeed, as we will see in chapter eleven, the last few years of the century witnessed a remarkable denominational "migration" of church members. Worship was, inevitably, affected.

The Jesus Movement

That the Jesus People might have been nothing more than the Church's answer to the hippies seems too obvious, too easy. True or not, we are hesitant to jump to that conclusion because the Church often follows after societal trends with "Johnny-come-lately" imitations; it's a sort of sanctified one-upmanship. Rather than this "clever" copying, the Jesus Movement and its Jesus People or Jesus Freaks was more a combination of converted hippies and young people from the traditional community of Christ-followers who were simply trying to be themselves in the context of being in the world, but not of it.

The slogan "One Way," so popular among the Jesus People, was more than an evangelistic endorsement of John 14:6. It proved to be a call to rise above and beyond denominationalism. "One Way" was not referring to one of the "ways" that had finally been proven to be "the" way. It was a call to leave the study of doctrine in the sanctuaries (the fort) in favor of taking the central biblical message to the street (the front), the central message boiled down and held up.

In its most noble expression, the message rose above normal generational differences. It was more profound than establishment versus anti-establishment issues. It was a test to see if the timeless message could move from tradition to radical reform one more time. Who from the sanctuary would follow the Jesus People and the gospel into the street? What from the sanctuary could be used in the street? What of established religion could survive the move from pew to curb, from altar to intersection? The Jesus People took the core message to the street to find out. They came back indoors, eventually, changed by what they had discovered outdoors. As these veterans of the front came back into the fort, zeal clashed with resolve. Worship styles were affected. Most often, discussions of "worship styles" are largely discussions of music styles and preferences.

Music changes when it takes to the street and so does worship. The move from the fort to the front presupposes an agenda. Music, in and of itself, can survive the move and the agendas. It is a pure art form that is often called upon to perform specific functions. Worship, however, upon assuming an agenda, ceases to be worship. It, by definition in the Christian context, exists for and is focused on adoration of God the Father, Son, and Holy Spirit. With an agenda, it changes from worship of God to a campaign for God. Campaigns in the name of justice and truth are biblical, Christian, and noble. They are acts of obedience, they are often the by-products of worship, but they are not worship.[4]

Front-line issues and concerns such as justice and peace are important biblical agendas for preaching and ministry action. They can strongly and properly inform worship. Involvement in these areas of ministry is energized by worship. Indeed, one might read Amos 5:21–24 and see them as prerequisites for worship. But no agenda, not even noble, biblical ones, should be allowed to occupy the throne with God (Exodus 20:3). To be sure, people need a place to stand in order to worship. Worshipers, by biblical decree, should be informed by, affected by, and fully aware of surrounding issues of justice and peace. But these issues are to be a part of the acknowledged environment in which worship takes place, not the *focus* of worship. If worship is to reveal and celebrate our relationship with God, it must reveal, before God, a relationship with one another that can be celebrated.[5] Focused on God, worship results in new passion and effectiveness in addressing the issues that are so urgent in the streets *and* the pews.

In their desire to take the *gospel* of Jesus to the streets as a tool, the Jesus People also took the *worship* of Jesus to the streets as a tool. The confusion of worship (a matter of the fort) with social action and protest (matters of the front) leads to tensions that can easily escalate into "war." Christians agree that God is worthy of worship. However, great difficulty comes in trying to agree on what issue, agenda, or need deserves a place next to God on Sunday morning.

The Jesus Movement's march from the fort to the front was meant to liberate the power of the gospel from its steepled prison.

---

[4]See introduction to *Part II: The War.*

[5]For further discussion and reflection on this concept, see Walter J. Burghardt, "Just Word and Just Worship: Biblical Justice and Christian Liturgy," in *Worship* 73:5 (September 1999).

However, some veterans of the fort saw the movement as an attempt to kidnap worship, perhaps to treat the Christian flag in the same way the American flag had been treated in the street. People will fight to protect what and whom they love. This is not to say that veterans of the fort were the guardians of pure worship and that those who went to the front were corrupting it. Both inside and outside of the fort, agendas were attached to worship. Agendas in worship are divisive. People are willing to go to war over agendas that have become heart-deep beliefs and convictions.

In his 1971 book, *The Jesus Trip,* Lowell Streiker described the Jesus People as ". . . young . . . zealous. They look like hippies. They have turned on to Jesus. They are as fanatic for the gospel as they once were for drugs and sex."[6] Many people saw these widespread and dramatic conversions as evidence of a revival; an important turning to God by a crucial segment of the American society. But, to a great extent, the revival and its converts were not welcome in existing congregations. Veterans of the fort were suspicious that the openness to drugs and sex had not been thoroughly washed away by the blood of the Lamb. They were not ready for Jesus to be seen as the next attempt at "escape." Though historically and doctrinally favorable toward evangelism, they were not ready to make Jesus popular, the stated aim of some in the Jesus Movement. Being turned on to Jesus as a substitute for being turned on to sex and drugs seemed blasphemous. This reluctance caused or freed the veterans of the front to build "new and improved" forts. This was an early mingling of fort and front mentality.

One of the most notable and enduring (still in existence) of the new forts was Calvary Chapel of Costa Mesa, Orange County, California. The following account, quoted earlier in the introduction, was not isolated:

> When I entered the University of California [Berkeley] I met the 'Jesus Movement,' a spiritual counterpart to the 1960s counterculture. I followed them to Calvary chapel in Costa Mesa, California, and witnessed something no Lutheran boy could imagine. It was a world of rock 'n' roll healing services in Hawaiian shirts, leather Bibles, and speaking in tongues in the thousands.[7]

---

[6]Lowell D. Streiker, *The Jesus Trip: Advent of the Jesus Freaks* (Nashville: Abingdon, 1971), 9.

[7]Gary M. Burge, "Missing God at Church?" *Christianity Today* 41:11 (October 6, 1997): 21ff.

Even so, Calvary Chapel proved to be one of the more sedate of the new youth-oriented congregations, often no more drastic in their innovation than the use of music of the contemporary folk style in their worship.

Others of the Jesus Movement's new forts such as the "Children of God," an outgrowth of the "American Soul Clinic, Inc.," and the "J.C. Light and Power House" were more fanatical. These were aggressive congregation/commune hybrids, that were more front than fort. After just two or three months of fundamentalist preaching, these young people, many from middle-class, church-going homes, had turned their backs on religion, to say nothing of denominations. However, they had given their hearts fully to Jesus.[8]

As avant-garde as these new forts of the organized front were, they were the work of adults. Mark Senter III cites this as the reason for the demise of the movement. He suggests that "The Jesus Movement of the 1960s, though short in duration, was a classic illustration of a spontaneous student movement . . . The movement died when well-meaning Christian adults began organizing the movement in behalf of youth."[9] We must be careful here. It should not be assumed that adults cannot do "front" work. His summation, though made in the context of the youth and adult generational differences, might also suggest that the work of the front can only remain effective as it stays free of the institutionalization of the fort. To the extent that this is true, it has significant implications in the context of the primary work of the front (evangelism) taking place within the primary work of the fort (worship).

The Jesus Movement was non-denominational. Members of several forts became veterans of the same front. They were different people, different worshipers when, having grown older and successful in business endeavors, they returned to their home forts. The potential for conflict was enormous. Their return was not perceived as the return of missionaries. Too often, it was the return of the rebels.

---

[8]For more information concerning these congregations and others like them, the author recommends James P. Wind and James W. Lewis, *American Congregations, Volume 1: Portraits of Twelve Religious Communities* (Chicago: University of Chicago Press, 1994).

[9]Mark Senter III, *The Coming Revolution in Youth Ministry* (Wheaton, Ill.: Victor, 1992), 51.

Billy Graham Crusades

Billy Graham, Baptist or Presbyterian? Reports and claims were made within both denominations from Montreat, North Carolina to Dallas, Texas. But, it didn't seem to matter. He was the spokesman for all evangelistic evangelicals. He was "every denomination" in evangelical and protestant circles.

Beginning with the 1949 Los Angeles crusade and continuing through the end of the twentieth century, Graham preached to hundreds of millions of people in cities all around the world. Indeed, his ministry continues into the twenty-first century. Each crusade was organized and promoted by many, if not all, of the local ministers and congregations in the host town or area.

> While many fundamentalists and evangelicals kept huddled in sectarian pride, Graham would refuse to come to your town unless there was broad "church federation" backing. He would not like to be on stage unless the United Methodist bishop or even, he has hoped since 1965 [Vatican II], the Catholic bishop was there, too. When people at his rallies converted or were restored or reaffirmed . . . he turned such folk over to the churches, and thus the church.[10]

Billy Graham was the preacher and his organization provided the structure. Very much at home in the fort and on the front, he was something of a "scout." The fire in his eyes rekindled the fire of the local pastors and revealed the presence of Christ in Dr. Graham's soul. The crowds encouraged the congregations. Evangelism could look like church. Veterans of the fort knew church. The crusades were big, successful church. Their dreams of growth (later to be formalized as "Church Growth") were possible. These were events and epiphanies that invigorated local congregations, whatever their denomination. For a week or so, Billy Graham was the city's preacher. He came, facilitated a moment of inter and intra-congregational cooperation, then left. It was good; not as threatening or as potentially lasting as local efforts at cross-denominational integration. "Billy" didn't care which local congregation his converts joined when he left. Indeed, a Billy Graham crusade invited all Christ-followers to experience the warmth of rising above earthly differences to experience a preview of heavenly unity. In the world of religious leadership, phrases like *The Left* and *The Right,*

---

[10]Martin E. Marty, "Reflections on Graham by a Former Grump," *Christianity Today* 32:17 (November 18, 1988): 24–25.

liberal or *conservative* mean less than *mean* and *non-mean,* and
Graham—to our great fortune—has been "nonmean."[11] A Billy
Graham crusade left a certain "taste" in the mouths of local Christians. The taste was good, a bit strange, yet recognizable. It was
the taste of living water from a common cup.

For veterans of the fort, Billy Graham represented the pastor
they thought they had hired this time and hoped to hire next time.
Though somewhat stuck in what they would come to call an old
paradigm, Billy Graham was also the grand old man of the veterans
of the front. At the same time, veterans of the fort saw what evangelistic preaching and a big choir could accomplish. Veterans of the
fort heard "Just As I Am" and veterans of the front heard "The New
23rd." Veterans of the front saw what current entertainment stars
and meeting outside the fort in "secular" venues could accomplish.
We do, indeed, see what we want to see. Whatever their focus,
those involved in Billy Graham crusades were experiencing a cross-
denominational phenomenon that was energizing and encouraging.

> He could have been a demagogue in these fateful decades [late
> '40s–late '80s]. . . . He could have formed formal coalitions with cor-
> rupting political forces, could have divided our Christian and national
> house, could have set us each against the other. He did not.[12]

In fact, Billy Graham's cross-denominational appeal opened some
minds and eyes, even if subconsciously. Christians were forced to
consider the possibility that Christ-followers from other traditions
were not strange cousins, but brothers and sisters.

Slowly, in some instances, more rapidly in others, worship
within local congregations was affected by what had been experienced at the Billy Graham crusade. Televising the crusades, of
course, accelerated and expanded all this. The music of the crusades was readily available to any and every congregation. It was a
powerful force as people left the stadium or turned off the TV and
returned to the local sanctuaries. The crusade soloists, Ethel
Waters and Bev Shea, were joined by guests. The guest soloists
were admired Christian recording artists whose denominational
ties were never mentioned and seldom known.

Within local communities and around the world, something of
a "Billy Graham globalization" was taking place. "Worlds" were
merging. War was looming.

---

[11] Ibid.
[12] Ibid.

Youth Musicals

Consideration of the youth musical phenomenon could well wait until chapter three, for the case can be made that they were a response by the fort to an innovation by the front—the para-church, traveling, young musical organizations. However, a quick focus on youth musicals is included here because of their cross-denominational or non-denominational acceptance and popularity. The youth musical was a major victory for the veterans of the front who were returning to the fort. For those more at home in the fort, the youth musical was a major concession fraught with risk. What would become of the classical, traditional repertory that prepared the young people for the adult choirs of the future? What would become of decorum and reverence in the sanctuary? Yet, the musicals afforded an opportunity for a bit of forward movement. Veterans could display something of an open-minded progressiveness as long as the guitars and drums could be kept under control.

Two youth musicals that are representative of the genre are *Good News,* compiled and arranged by Bob Oldenburg (1967) and *Tell It Like It Is,* composed by Ralph Carmichael and Kurt Kaiser (1969). Both works claimed the designation "folk musical" on the cover. Indeed, the early youth musicals were more "folk" than "pop" . . . fortunately in that, "folk" was the more acceptable term inside the fort. It is important to note here that *Good News* was published by a denominational publishing house, the Southern Baptist Broadman Press. *Tell It Like It Is* was published by the non-denominational, yet Christian company, Lexicon Music, Incorporated of Waco, Texas. The significance of this non-denominational involvement will be considered later. Let it suffice here to simply remind ourselves, that non-denominational publishing houses were not controlled by ecclesial judicatories, or their doctrines. To focus on one denomination, however, many of the composers and publishers in the "commercial" houses were Southern Baptist.

The youth musicals were bold. Their music was from the front, yet their "book and lyrics" were from the core message of the fort. Unapologetic use of guitars and drums was coupled with measured staging instructions such as the following for presentation of the "I'm a Rebel" song in *Good News:*

Dress four youth in "hippie" attire. long hair, dark glasses, sweat shirts, dirty jeans; one with a guitar strapped to his back, two carrying picket signs reading, "Peace" and "Amen." Do not dress them ridiculously or offensively, but set the mood.[13]

If the congregation was somewhat unsettled at this point, relief and reassurance were on the way. The quartet of "rebels," declaring they are "headed in the other way," is immediately rebuffed by the more acceptably clad (though not in choir robes) balance of the youth choir. With the look and sound of the front, they represent the fort as they sing "We're gonna change this land . . . led by God's own hand."[14] Should the congregation be relieved or worried?

Carefully staged, carefully instructed, looking very "mod" and sounding a bit like "Peter, Paul, and Mary," rapidly growing youth choirs performed within the fort and out on the front. That, in and of itself, was good. Veterans of the fort could not speak against innovative evangelism, and they certainly were pleased that their young people were involved and active in the church. Guitars, drums, and street clothes instead of robes could be somewhat contained in safe areas such as fellowship halls, Sunday nights, and youth events. But, like all kids, the youth choir didn't always wipe their feet when they came back into the house. Nor did they forget the "fun" they had outside. As they advanced from high school into college and young adulthood, their influence in the church increased, as well it should have.

In 1975, Southern Baptists, like many other denominations in the same general time frame, replaced their existing hymnal. The 1975 book replaced their hymnal of 1956. The new hymnal contained Bill Cates' "Do You Really Care?" . . . one of the songs in *Good News.* This was not the only new "hymn" from a youth musical. Veterans of the fort and veterans of the front disagreed on the appropriateness of this innovation. Although *Baptist Hymnal,* 1975 was widely and enthusiastically received, some congregations chose to stay with the 1956 hymnal and its "better quality of music."

Baptist Hymnal, 1975 also included Baptist composer Kurt Kaiser's new hymn "Pass It On" from the youth folk musical *Tell It*

---

[13] Bob Oldenburg, *Good News: A Christian Folk Musical* (Nashville: Broadman, 1967), unnumbered p. 7

[14] "We're Gonna Change This Land," words by Frank Hart Smith and Ted Overman, music by Johnny Fullerton from *Good News* (see above), 55–56.

Like It Is.[15] Youth choirs moved from the final performance of one musical to rehearsals for the next. *Tell It Like It Is* was certainly on the list of "must do" musicals. The list did not distinguish between denominational and non-denominational publishers.

There are some interesting differences between the two representative musicals we are considering. Both musicals suggest only modest drama in the presentation. In fact, while *Good News* does include basic "Suggestions for Performance," the Carmichael/Kaiser work has no such instructions and only the barest of suggested dialogue sparsely positioned throughout the book. Yet, both encourage the choir to do something other than stand in the choir loft. Indeed, in the short time between 1967 and 1969, ministers of music had become quite adept at "staging" musicals, replicating "front" activity within the fortified confines of their sanctuary and congregational tolerances. Indeed, youth choirs often left the fort and took their musicals out to the front. Youth choir tours, though not always "mission trips," gave the children of the fort a taste of the front.

While the score of *Good News* (and others of the early musicals) looked as different from conventional choral music as it sounded (approx. 8 1/2" x 12"), the trim size of *Tell It Like It Is* (approx. 6 1/2" x 10") was more recognizable to seasoned ministers of music and adult choir members who might take notice. *Tell It Like It Is* looked like it could have been a John Peterson seasonal cantata. Admittedly, this may be a minor point at best, especially since these musicals were most often memorized for performance. But it does speak to the fact that the youth musical was fitting in. For veterans of the fort, it looked like the singers of youth musicals could easily fit traditional music into their choir folders when they grew up. For young veterans of the front, their was an unspoken resolve that their "new" music would always "fit in the folders." Why change at a particular age? For many, there would be neither need nor inclination to revert in the future.

Tell It Like It Is did more than help link the new ("contemporary" is not yet a key word) youth musical with the traditional hymnal and congregational song. One of its several memorable songs was Ralph Carmichael's "Love Is Surrender." Its "pop" sound was no different than what could be heard on the youth-oriented radio stations. It was fresh and very "now." So in tune was it with the

---

[15]Ralph Carmichael and Kurt Kaiser, *Tell It Like It Is: A Folk Musical for Choir and Solos* (Waco, Tex.: Lexicon Music, 1969), 123.

secular sound of the day, it was recorded (with minor word changes) by the hit brother and sister duo The Carpenters. Further testimony to this song's popularity is the fact that is was subsequently used by a jewelry company in nation-wide television advertisements for diamond wedding rings. In 1976, Ralph Carmichael and the Lexicon company released (published) *The New Church Hymnal,* a non-denominational collection that included, "Love Is Surrender." What has been presented here is but one evidence that youth musicals, congregational song, denominational and non-denominational hymnals, and commercial television had discernable, even if coincidental, linkages. Veterans of both sorts marked their "maps." Ground had been taken.

THREE

Para-church Youth Movement

While I can name distinct practices of
church, I cannot see them anywhere except
as they are expressed in particular cultural
forms of actual congregations.

Thomas Edward Frank[1]

"Movement" was a popular word in the 1960s and early 1970s. The "Jesus Movement," already discussed, located the church's struggles with radical change squarely in the mix of other upheavals.

> Later that month [January, 1971] NBC ran a national television news story on the Jesus Movement, as did CBS in April. During the first week in February *Look* magazine featured a cover article in which it was announced, "The Jesus Movement is upon us . . . It shows every sign . . . of becoming a national preoccupation."[2]

In 1971, the Jesus movement was named the news event of the year in religion by the Religion News Writers Association. The very word, "movement" suggests change, forward thinking, motivation and purposeful migration. It was happening on many fronts. There was a peace movement, a civil rights movement, an "anti-establishment" movement and others less widespread in their influence. There was a Christian youth movement as well and it had both fort and front manifestations.

---

[1] *The Soul of the Congregation: An Invitation to Congregational Reflection* (Nashville: Abingdon, 2000), 54.

[2] Billy Graham, *The Jesus Generation* (Minneapolis: World Wide Publications, 1971), 14–15.

Youth Ministers

Inside the fort, youth "ministries" were established, directed by new staff members called "Youth Ministers," "Youth Pastors," or "Ministers of Youth." These were young adults employed and placed on the ministerial staff for one or more of several reasons. Moving from less noble to more noble, the reasons included attempts to manage the emerging youth culture within the fort by means of an accountable staff position and to compete with larger congregations that had added the position and ministry. Further, some congregations saw this ministerial staff position as a logical next step in a progression that had begun with Junior High School and Senior High School Sunday School classes and moved through youth fellowship meetings. Hiring a "Youth Pastor" was an acknowledgement that the needs of teenagers (a relatively new term) needed to be addressed on a full-time basis. The Sunday responsibilities of the Senior Pastor were focused, largely, on matters pertaining to adult-oriented worship planning and leadership. Would it not follow, then that the Youth Pastor or Youth Minister, armed with staff status, would have similar responsibilities for his or her young "congregation"? Youth were staying in and coming in to the life of the church in droves. So closely was music tied to this movement, many congregations hired "Ministers of Music and Youth," combining an established position with a new one. This combination position also came about because many congregations did not, in fact, have the money or the young people to support a full-time "ministry" dedicated only to the young people. Using the youth musicals mentioned in the previous chapter and the youth mission trip (often combined with a concert tour), youth ministries were growing at phenomenal rates. Veterans of the fort could not have been happier. When the newly established or lately enlivened youth choirs sang, the young people dressed alike. While the older veterans may not have appreciated the uniforms, they certainly appreciated the uniformity. Having given up on "conformity" in a frightening world of "doing your own thing," they gladly settled for the colorful uniformity. The "kids" were busy inside the walls of the fort, rather than hanging around out in the parking lot. They were in sight, not on drugs, active in Sunday School, choir, and mission trips. Rooms or suites within the existing facilities, even entire new buildings, were dedicated to the youth activities. What they were doing was different, and, relatively speaking, only mildly rebellious, but youth groups would not be denied the worship that matched the movement. They had a pastor, someone much nearer the age of junior and senior high students than the senior pastor, organizing and overseeing all this. Parents, frustrated at attempts to keep their teenagers in church, had help from someone who was naturally "relevant," the Minister of Youth. The youth pastor was a powerful person, even when the power was kept sheathed. There was a flurry of activity and growth within local congregations as youth ministries bought vans, buses, and sound equipment. Soon their choir was no longer the "youth" choir (as opposed to the "adult choir"). They became "The New Life Singers," or some similar title. The trajectory of continued relevance and influence didn't stop at high school graduation. As they entered college they became "Tapestry." However, returning to the fort after college, they were faced with joining the adult choir if they were to continue singing. The adult choir hadn't changed much while they were gone. Nor had the adult worship environment that they had escaped as "youth" within the fort. Change would come to many choirs and worship environments within the fort. Battles were brewing.

Para-church Youth Ministries

Why the new names and outfits for the youth choir? Why specific ministries, ministers, and meeting rooms? There was a movement afoot out on the front, and it was, or at least was capable of, pulling the youth away from the church. It was not so much new as it was newly energized. Though Christian, it operated outside of and apart from the fort. Several organizations, separate but similar, constituted the "Christian youth movement" of the 1960s and 1970s. They were variations of the existing model/foundation of "Youth for Christ."

> About the same time that the NAE [National Association of Evangelicals, founded 1943] was beginning to give religious conservatism a national identity, another movement called Youth for Christ was starting to give evangelicalism an articulate voice among the nation's high school students. Its method followed that of the great urban revivalists of the late nineteenth century. On Memorial Day, 1945, for example, it packed 70,000 people into Chicago's Soldier Field for a day

of open-air preaching, commemoration of fallen servicemen, gospel music, testimonies, and rededication to the evangelical cause.[3]

Note the conservative and nationalistic facets of the event just described. For some congregations this was fully in keeping with their orientations. Certainly the World War II-related patriotism was understood at that time in our history and now. But not all congregations were so conservative. Not all congregations were so eager to weave Christian zeal and national patriotism into the same fabric. Those hesitancies, however isolated they may have been in the '40s, certainly became much more widespread in the '60s when the traditional concepts of war and patriotism were severely challenged, and beyond.

Youth for Christ was not the only organization of its type to emerge during and just after World War II, but it can be argued that it was the most influential. Though Youth for Christ remained strong over the decades, its para-church (outside the fort) structure, as mentioned earlier, seemed to be rediscovered as a model in the 1970s.

> By the middle of the decade [1970s], the only Jesus movement that mattered much was made up of middle-class young people. Young Life, Campus Crusade, the Navigators, the InterVarsity Fellowship, and various denominational groups attracted the young.[4]

"Youth movements, like Youth for Christ, were widely hailed as effective means of drawing young people into the churches."[5] Yet, their youth-oriented rallies, attendance, and energy could seldom be matched within the fort. The youth ministries mentioned earlier began to sprout in local congregations, but it took some time (if it ever happened) for those focused efforts to have similar drawing power. Indeed, as a sort of truce or in attempts to capitalize on their energy, Ministers of Youth often encouraged and accompanied young church members' attendance at these "extra-fort" events. Para-church youth gatherings, large or small, rallies and Bible studies, included times of "worship." Youth-generated music, instruments, perspectives, and energy, and freedom from

---

[3] Robert Wuthnow, *The Restructuring of American Religion: Society and Faith Since World War II* (Princeton, N.J.: Princeton University Press, 1988), 175.

[4] Martin E. Marty, *Pilgrims in Their Own Land: 500 Years of Religion in America* (New York: Penguin, 1984), 469.

[5] Wuthnow, 18.

the adults and trappings of the fort characterized these worship experiences. Preaching, too, was young and "with it."

While some young people were able to balance their involvement in youth ministries of both the front and the fort, others only grew more discontent with the sluggishness and more limited vision of the smaller local church youth ministries. Regional groups of churches from particular denominations began gathering their congregational youth groups into large "rallies" on Saturday nights, perhaps once a month or once a quarter. This was a sort of middle-ground between the para-church events and the less satisfying attempts of an individual local congregation. Southern Baptists called their version "Associational Youth Rallies." In many cases, however, the youth ministers accepted the challenge of matching, in their local congregational setting, the environment and energy of the para-church and regional denominational rallies. Larger congregations were often able to more closely replicate the para-church events.

Youth-led worship services within the traditional congregational setting were influenced by the music and worship of the youth movement, pushing and pulling at the traditional format, but these were often once-a-quarter events. This was not often enough for many youth ministers and their charges, so they obtained permission to conduct youth worship services away from the sanctuary, in the youth building or the basement. Each week on Sunday nights, if not on Sunday mornings, the local church youth ministry could try again to match the para-church events. Many in the fort felt that they had to grant this separation in order to keep or reclaim the youth. Worthy attempts, understandable concerns and motivations, but one day the youth would grow into adulthood and congregational leadership.

In addition to the organizations that held Bible studies and rallies within a fixed geographic region, there were traveling para-church "youth choirs" or ensembles. One of the earliest and most influential of these youth music groups, "Up With People," was actually a secular organization, but carried messages of peace, love and brotherhood. It identified and encouraged what was right with American teenagers. They highlighted what was perceived to be the brighter and more positive aspects of the youth culture. "Up With People" singers were young, attractive, and energetic, yet, in uniform . . . a not-so-subtle signal to the establishment that this was neither chaos nor rebellion. Granted, their uniforms were "mod" (modern), but uniform nonetheless, and neat. They could be trusted to a point by veterans of the fort. At the same time, their very existence, moderate choreography, and music brought hope (and ideas) to veterans of the front. For some congregations, this was acceptable. For others, "Up With People" would have to be "baptized" before it could be granted additional trust and good-will. "Up With People" gave concerts and recorded their music, all outside the fort and without the front's message.

Similar groups, equally as popular, such as "Truth" and "The Continental Singers" began to be organized and were openly and purposefully Christian. Some of the Christian groups had their origins within the fort's youth choirs. Their leaders had exceptional compositional, organizational, and entrepreneurial skills. These groups sang in concerts, made recordings, and lent their names to published collections of their music, collections to be purchased by the youth choirs back in the fort.

"Up With People" was clean, neat, polite, and American. "Truth" and "The Continental Singers" were all that, plus openly Christian. Youth choirs were all that and safely within the fort. It seems strange that the church, whether in its fort or front modalities, would find it necessary to have a "Christian version" of a secular musical group that was organized for the good of society. Yet, it isn't so strange. The church has often adopted society's creative ideas for the added purpose of spreading the gospel, asking, "Why didn't we think of that first?" It is an understandable and often commendable response. Whether secular or Christian, the para-church youth ensembles raised the bar high above the heads of the local congregation youth choirs. Many youth choirs of the fort rose to the challenge, took what they *could* do and "hit the road" to sing and "do" the gospel. These were wonderful experiences for the young people of the fort. However, the musical repertory and freedom of form in their musical evangelism would follow them back into the fort's worship via the home concert at the end of the tour, youth-led worship services, and youth choir presentations on Sunday nights. It would soon be discovered that when the children of the fort out-grew the youth choir, youth choir tours, and youth worship services, they would not out-grow their love of the repertory nor of the freshness and freedom they had encountered in these worship and worship-*esque* events.

Would the "youth group" have to be continued into its adult-hood in order to keep within the fort those who had experienced even short excursions to the front? What would it take to bring them back into the fort? Some veterans of the fort converted to the worship of the front, finding it somehow fresh and freeing. Others surrendered, tolerating the changes in order to be with the younger people during the worship hour. Others fought. It is not correct to assume, however, that all teenagers were, by virtue of their age, soldiers of the front. Some of the young people entering adulthood and related church responsibilities, never left the fort, physically nor philosophically.

The church was drawing ever closer to worship war. In years to come, battles would be fought over congregational song, the existence of choirs, the structure of worship, the purpose of worship, and where the line is drawn between reform and rejection. The youth had found in the para-church Christian youth movement something akin to what older veterans (both fort and front) had found in Billy Graham's crusades. They would not forget the experience of finding worship "outside" and bringing it in. They would not forget the larger experience of worshiping with Christians of other denominations. Indeed, they would not forget non-denominational Christianity.

Part II

THE WAR

FOUR

The Politicization of Worship

*At no point in the witness of the Church to the
world is its integrity as a reconciled society more
radical and more cogent than in the liturgy.*

William Stringfellow[1]

Worship Styles

The decades of the 1970s and 1980s saw shifts in focus within
worship. While Roman Catholics continued to struggle with the
application of Vatican II decrees, mainline Protestants and evangelicals had in-house struggles of their own. For as long as one could
remember, free-church pastors had instructed (directly and indi-
rectly) their Ministers of Music to "put the worship service together
and let me know when its time to preach." Despite feeling in their
souls and learning in their seminaries that worship planning should
be a team effort, the Minister of Music was left to do the job alone.
In traditions where the lectionary was not followed, this situation
often led to the Minister of Music guessing as to what "direction" the
worship service was going to take. Fortunate was the Minister of
Music whose pastor would outline sermon titles and Scripture passages for six months, even six weeks into the future. When such
advance planning did take place, the action was, in fact, the creation of little parish-sized "lectionaries," though those involved
would never have confessed that that was the case.

It was during this time that worship became a hot topic;
so too, did the politics of power within several Christian traditions. The discussion that follows is focused on "in-house" or theo-
political issues. The church in its hour of worship stands strongly

---

[1] *Dissenter in a Great Society: A Christian View of America in Crisis*
(New York: Holt, Rinehart & Winston, 1966), 150.

and overtly to declare that its citizenship in the kingdom of heaven
takes precedent over temporary citizenship here in the kingdom of
this world. The church's positioning of itself within the kingdom
of heaven is, indeed, a political, even subversive act. "Worship in
a congregation that gathers to acknowledge its Lord and seek
his will and direction is thus supremely a political event."[2] "In
short, wherever a congregation is found, it must be a colony of
heaven. . . ."[3] Worship is a political event. This awareness should
serve to unite the church, especially in post "Christendom." But,
Christian against Christian political in-fighting ("friendly fire," to
put it in warfare terminology) in the context of worship flared and
proved divisive.

In-house theo-political power struggles, though not limited to
them, were nowhere more obvious and intense than among Southern Baptists in the final few decades of the twentieth century. The
emergence of worship and politics as simultaneous, but separate,
volatile issues was most interesting. The subject of worship was
becoming financially profitable and, as we shall see later, was sol-
idly linked to "church growth." At the same time, theological debate
was realizing a new political currency. Worship was selling books
and filling newly birthed conferences. Pastors became interested in
the worship planning process. Ministers of Music extended a wary
welcome. Theological debate (including the theology of worship)
was producing a vocabulary or arsenal of "word-weapons." Strategies for takeover and forced power shifts rivaled the best efforts of
field grade officers and generals. From the smallest congregations to
the highest judicatory levels, worship and church-related vocabulary changes were forced with little or no regard for "civilian casualties" (death of those who were not members of the competing
armies). The changes in worship were to evangelize the "un-
churched" and reclaim the "once-churched." Forced vocabulary
changes were to theologically "right" the "old ship of Zion," thought
by the newly empowered to be listing to the port side.

---

[2]George W. Webber, *The Congregation in Mission* (Nashville: Abingdon, 1964), 93. Certainly, many other writers attest to this fact. Among the
more notable of recent times is Marva J. Dawn. See citation above.

[3]Howard G. Hageman, "The Theology of the Urban Church," in *Cities and Churches: Readings on the Urban Church* (ed. Robert Lee; Philadelphia: Westminster, 1962), 339. Again, many recent writers have put
forth this same understanding. The author includes copyrights from the
1960s to show that the subject was being debated even during the time
that political unrest was being experienced within the church.

Verbal and musical vocabularies quickly defined the positions of persons and congregations within the conflict. Worship styles waved like banners atop steeples. The terms "high church" and "low church" no longer adequately described differences in worship practices. Those simple terms were the coincidental and friendly designations of a time suddenly relegated to history. Five or six style-labels became necessary to accommodate the newly important designations. But, for ease of carrying into battle, these several worship styles could be grouped into two convenient backpacks: traditional and contemporary.

The theo-political war stockpiled its arsenal of word-weapons by first re-tooling conservative and moderate into fundamentalist and liberal, then, high and low into funeral and circus.

In the 1960s it was not uncommon for congregations to reconsider their ministry and outreach efforts, even the content and/or structure of their worship in light of significant social issues within the American culture. These were "political" issues in as much as they challenged social injustices of several types and the governance that created or sustained them. They were the politics, inside and outside the fort, of ministry. Referring to his time as pastor of the Church of St. John the Baptist, a congregation in the Bronx, Paul C. Carter wrote in 1967:

> Soon, however, we began to get used to the idea that so-called "worldly concerns" have a very real place in worship. . . . At times we invited local civic leaders to speak to us on local neighborhood problems during this section of worship. . . . We are deeply sorry that changes in our worship life have cost us members. We also miss the sense of spiritual tranquility which was present before we began discussing worldly matters in our concern section of worship. But these changes have brought us a new understanding that true worship involves serving our neighbor, and this we appreciate.[4]

In the following decades, however, the church's political activity turned more toward posturing than ministry. In the 1970s and 1980s (not so much so in the 1990s) if a congregation chose praise as their worship style, one could assume that they were conservative on all matters of theology, social issues, denominational and national politics. Likewise, a liturgical worship style meant liberal stances in those same categories. The situation might well have

---

[4]Paul C. Carter Jr., "The Changing Face of a Church," in *The Church Creative* (ed. M. Edward Clark et al.; Nashville: Abingdon, 1967), 48–49.

been described by what is now one of America's new war phrases, a "war of images." The styles "in between" were variations viewed as either friend or foe, depending on one's vantage point. Style migration carried theo-political significance. For example, a congregational move from a traditional worship style to the "blended" designation was considered a cautious move to the "right," not the "left." In truth, a move toward "blended" may well have only been an attempt to test the reported church-growth effectiveness of praise choruses and contemporary worship.

Interestingly, like old generals in the rear echelon sending young privates to the front, preachers, *"generally"* speaking, did not adjust their style of sermon preparation or delivery as new worship styles were employed. They often insisted that the church musicians follow the fads or carry the banner of newness and relevance on behalf of the pastoral leadership team. Certainly, there were exceptions in which the minister of music raced far ahead of the pastor and congregation or, conversely, refused to move at all.

To be fair, a number of pastors found a freshness in moving from the "three-points-and-a-poem" method to "narrative" preaching styles, sharing in the risk of change. In large measure, however, pastors only changed uniforms, removing coat and tie for the contemporary service, while church musicians re-tooled choirs, instrumentation, congregational song repertory and methodology, and leadership decorum. This put the minister of music "on the point" as the worship wars moved into unfamiliar territory. Staff meetings and worship planning often became occasions for "fire fights."

War, especially war without clearly defined front lines, objectives, and enemies is confusing. Motivations and levels of enthusiasm for changing or retaining worship/musical styles often differed significantly, even within a local congregation. This became dangerously confusing. Ministers of music and pastors were attempting to hold on to core values and be relevant at the same time; to grow the church, maintain some recognizable tradition, and "stay alive," that is to say, keep their jobs. This called for political maneuvering, and, as in any conflict, clear and efficient communication. Unfortunately, the political maneuvering was often more prevalent than the communication. Many ministers of music and some pastors lost their positions due to this "friendly fire."

The politicization of worship was not confined to the church's congregations and judicatory agencies. Church-affiliated institutions of higher education have traditionally argued over whether or not "chapel" should be a worship event or a "lab" experiment and who should be in charge, students or faculty. However, the worship wars brought a new significance to the winner of the argument. Here is testimony reported by Ted Peters:

> Seminary chapel has become politicized. Worship has become the arena for establishing group spirit among those who advocate a decisive position on the politically correct hot topics. Whenever a controversy breaks out in the church some group or another plans a worship service in which one side blesses its own position by appeal to symbols of ultimacy.[5]

It is a sad day when a seminary becomes a "boot-camp" for any other war than the one that is fought against "the cosmic powers of this present darkness, against the spiritual forces of evil in the heavenly places" (Eph 6:12, NRSV).

New Hymnals and Money

> As a source of courage, people charge to music, march to music, and cheer with music. It intensifies emotions, unifies beliefs, and accompanies actions. This same potential for positive action becomes a banner of loyalty and war.[6]

If this quote is true for particular songs, and it is, then its truth only intensifies when songs are gathered together in a hymnal. This is especially true when the hymnal bears the name of the denomination that published it. Denominational hymnals are duty-bound to reflect the doctrines of their constituency. Further, they must include the musical styles that are acceptable to that constituency for both ethical and economic reasons.

The more diversified the worship styles, doctrinal verities, and political stances within the denomination, the more difficult it is to produce their hymnal. Further, if a congregation is at odds with its denominational hierarchy over any of those issues, there is no better way to declare the difference, exert independence, or exercise defiance than to adopt and purchase a "different" hymnal.

Non-denominational or "commercial" hymnals are not obligated to adhere to the doctrinal or musical characteristics of any

---

[5] Ted Peters, "Worship Wars," *Dialog* 33, no. 3 (1994): 167.

[6] J. Nathan Corbitt, *The Sound of the Harvest: Music's Mission in Church and Culture* (Grand Rapids: Baker, 1998), 89–90.

given denomination. Their hymnal development committees are often much smaller and, thus more nimble than those of denominational projects. They are freer to follow related trends or to establish new ones. In the worship wars, non-denominational publishers were able to engage in market-niche focusing. This is not to imply that the publishers of non-denominational hymnals were irresponsible or careless, nor that publishers of denominational hymnals were non-responsive. Non-denominational hymnal publishers were, and are, Christians in business. However, while denominational publishing houses are indeed Christians in business, they are also extensions of their constituent congregations. Operations within denominational publishing houses were and are often more cumbersome than in the smaller, non-denominational companies. Wherever they are produced, hymnals have the potential to be big moneymakers. Like any business venture, they can fail. But when a hymnal is a "success" it is a boon for its publisher.

Non-denominational hymnals have been around for a long time. In fact, for many years, non-denominational hymnals were the only ones available. One need only look to the collections of Isaac Watts beginning in early eighteenth-century England for examples. When denominational hymnals came on the scene in America during the nineteenth century, they did not take over "the market," but they certainly had impact and extra-musical significance. They helped define, declare, and teach a denomination's doctrine. Denominational hymnals functioned as something of a doctrinal statement, galvanizing denominational identity. It is easy to see then, that the decision to use a hymnal other than the one produced by your denomination can be interpreted as a clear and potent statement of defiance, if not mutiny, even if the contents are quite similar.

Pew racks contained evidence that the distant rumblings were not thunder. The acceptance of "commercial" hymnals had financial implications and fed fears of a breaking of the ranks. Still others, those who wished to break away from the worship styles "suggested" by the contents of their existing denominational hymnals, had, in the non-denominational hymnals of the 1970s and 1980s, a formidable arsenal for the worship wars at hand.

It must be re-emphasized, however, that the production of new hymnals was logical during that time. Congregations were ready to discard some congregational songs of the fort and add some of the front. That, in and of itself, was not an "act of war." Authors and composers of church music and the emerging Christian music industry were producing fresh expressions for those on the leading edge of worship reform. Reform need not be revolution. Veterans of the fort and veterans of the front do, in fact, salute a common flag.

Even though they sensed the need for a new hymnal at the same time the denominational companies did, the "commercial" hymnals often moved more swiftly, filling congregational worship "niches," both contemporary and traditional. This made the denominational houses look like they were playing "follow the leader." But this was no game. Even though the producers of the several hymnals were friends, colleagues, and fellow Christians, their products were often and soon drafted into a war with theological, financial, and worship fronts. The battlefield was the local congregation. Denominational loyalty protected fewer and fewer pew racks. The potential for financial windfalls produced more and more "ammunition." No doubt, some hymnals came into being for the purpose of exploiting popular copyrights (songs). Yet, in all of this, there were soldiers at every level who were "fighting" for the cause of enriched worship, whatever the secondary ramifications might have been. Indeed, there was significant sharing of information (for free) and copyrights (for a fee) among the friends and colleagues within and across the denominational/ non-denomination lines.

Nevertheless, the timing and intensity of hymnal publishing activity was evidence of the intensity of the worship wars that raged throughout American Christianity. Notice the following publication dates of denominational and non-denominational hymnals:

- *Hymns for the Living Church* (Hope, 1974)
- *Baptist Hymnal* (1975)
- *The New Church Hymnal* (Lexicon, 1976)
- *Hymns for the Family of God* (Paragon, 1976)
- *Lutheran Book of Worship* (1978)
- *The Hymnal 1982* (Episcopal)
- *The Singing Church* (Hope, 1985)
- *Worship III* (Catholic, 1986)
- *The Hymnal for Worship and Celebration* (Word, 1986)
- *Psalter Hymnal* (CRC, 1987)
- *Worship His Majesty* (Gaither, 1987)
- *The United Methodist Hymnal* (1989)

A similar publication pattern continued into the 1990s. It should be noted that *Worship III,* included in the listing above, was immune to the competition of non-denominational hymnals, but not to social and liturgical influences. It is included to emphasize the fact that the legitimate need for new hymnals was universal throughout the Christian community.

It is a fact, even if conceded begrudgingly, that wars produce positive advances in important technologies. Even in the bloodless worship wars there were developments seen by many as advances in the "technology" of worship. The word "technology" here refers not only to audio, visual, and soon electronic matters, but also to the types of songs considered appropriate for inclusion in hymnals.

The songs of popular "Christian artists" (see chapter five) quickly found their way from performance hall, radio, and music stores to the choir loft and the hymnal (most quickly and heavily in the non-denominational books). For veterans of the front this was a wonderful advance in worship; a victory. For veterans of the fort, it was something to be carefully considered, even resisted.

Wartime technology took the hymns and projected them on a large screen above and/or behind the choir, in front of the baptistry. Hymnals, no matter their publisher, often stayed in the pew racks while hymns appeared and disappeared before the worshipers' very eyes. Did the non-hymnic contents of the hymnals not matter (a question previously asked when creeds appeared in some non-denominational hymnals in evangelical pew racks)? Veterans of the front cheered the chance to lift hands and eyes, to connect with a generation used to television screens, movie screens, and, increasingly, computer screens. Veterans of the fort wondered about the priesthood of the believer if the hymnal and all of its contents were taken from their hands by those calling the shots up front on the "stage." In many "theaters" of the war, hymnals were casualties.

FIVE

Christian Popular Music

*Basically there can be no categories such
as "religious" art and "secular" art
because all true art is incarnational,
and therefore "religious."*

Madeleine L'Engle[1]

The Music and the Christian Artist

I recall how pleased many Christians were when they discovered that Tom Netherton of the "Lawrence Welk Show" was a brother in Christ. Tennessee Ernie Ford and, later, Andy Griffith were even better known. They recorded hymns and occasionally sang them on their television shows. This was not a threat to the veterans of the fort. In fact, it seemed a special victory to know that celebrities shared Christian kinship and testimony, shared our songs. It was a validation of sorts, a connection. "Cousin Ern" was our brother. Andy knew what we knew. Great confusion and consternation arose, however, when Elvis Presley began to record hymns. To many veterans of the fort he was, perhaps, an affront, if not a threat. But, questions about Elvis aside, these were celebrities who just happened to be Christian.

Christian celebrities singing "our songs" gave veterans of the front some creative ideas. Why not compose Christian popular songs specifically designed to join the religious folksongs and hymns that were already on the stage and in the studios? The idea seemed so right and irresistible, why not also "create" Christian artists (vs. artists who are Christian) to sing these songs? Still, only the most skittish would have imagined any kind of threat to the fort or

---

[1] *Walking on Water: Reflections on Faith and Art* (Wheaton, Ill.: Harold Shaw, 1998), 27.

its veterans. There was the stage and there was the sanctuary. Society knew they were separate venues. Everyone knew the difference and the boundaries. The twain, however, were to meet. It would mean war.

A note of caution should be sounded before we continue. The Christian popular music of our time should not be seen as a new idea. There is a long history of the music of the people being "discovered," and "baptized into Christianity," certainly long before Vatican II. It was the remarkable advancements in technology and the social environment surrounding America's worship wars that gave the recurring cycle unique charm and unobstructed inroads this time around.

> Contemporary Christian music may not have started in the church, But its profound impact on the church is undeniable, said a music industry executive. "In the annals of sacred music history, this type of expression is unprecedented in its growth and popularity," said John Styll, president of Nashville-based CCM Communications and chairman-elect of the Gospel Music Association.[2]

Now we continue. Why do we sense a special victory for the church when Christian recording artists and their music make the same money, share the same spotlight, receive the same Gold Records, Grammys, etc. as secular performers? Perhaps it is seeing Christian music recognized as equally artistic when compared to the more serious or "relevant" popular music of the day. Such recognition can be seen as a new level of achievement for evangelism. It can be seen as a unique platform for sharing one's Christian testimony. For some, it is seen almost as a victory won for Jesus . . . certainly for his music.

If Christian music is accomplishing such wonderful feats out on the popular front, why not bring it home to the fort? From whom should we seek recognition and acceptance? Is not the desire for human recognition a characteristic of the "old self" to which we have died? Are not the Christian artist and Christian popular music merely extensions of the established and accepted Minister of Music and church music ministry? The dialogue these

---

[2]John Styll, "Worship and Music," Lecture, Golden Gate Baptist Theological Seminary, Mill Valley, California, April 5, 2001, quoted in Cameron Crabtree, "Music Exec Notes: Impact of Contemporary Music," *Gateway: Golden Gate Baptist Theological Seminary Magazine for Alumni and Friends* (Spring 2001): 7.

questions represent took place in formal and informal discussions within the fort. Accompanying emotions rose to the surface and fueled the worship wars.

What about the suggestion that entertainment industry recognitions and awards open a new and vast arena for sharing the gospel? True to a certain extent, the full potential for taking the gospel to the unchurched via highly professional Christian music has not been met. How many non-Christians listen to Christian music? Certainly some did and do. Like any evangelistic or missionary strategy, it falls short of doing the job by itself. Further, the likelihood of effectiveness increases when one considers the "cross-over" artists to be bridges between the Christian and secular recording industries.

Even if the non-Christian audience is relatively small, the thinking goes, Christian artists and their music give "our kids" something to listen to other than the drastically non-Christian lyrics of secular popular music. This is especially effective when the Christian music is comparable to secular pop music in style, artistry, and quality. Commenting on the popularity of Contemporary Christian and "crossover" singing artist Amy Grant, Todd Gold wrote in *The Saturday Evening Post,* "her songs have given religion a catchy rhythm, and more than a few parents have been known to rejoice, 'Thank the Lord for this little lady.'"[3] And here we are back at the Grammy awards ceremony.

So, after a very short trip we have arrived at valid reasons for the existence of Christian popular music. In this context, celebrity and equality in the secular arena can be seen as valuable tools in evangelism and discipleship. Acknowledging the positive aspects of Christian entertainment, we will stop short of entering the question of what makes art "Christian." Madeline L'Engle has already done an excellent job of boiling that question down for us.[4] We return to Christian popular music and how it has contributed to the Church's worship wars.

When the Christian music of the popular music front was brought to the fort an important question entered the fray. How entertaining should worship be . . . especially now that Christianity

---

[3] Todd Gold, "Amy Grant: Music From the Heart," *The Saturday Evening Post* (May/June 1986): 43–45.

[4] Madeline L'Engle, *Walking on Water: Reflections on Faith and Art* (Wheaton, Ill.: Harold Shaw, 1998). For specific focus on this matter, see chapter two, "Icons of the True."

had its own popular music and artists? With a spectacular show on one extreme and mind-numbing boredom on the other, we stood at various places in the middle searching for an answer. Answers, when arrived at, would declare one's alliance with either the veterans of the front or the veterans of the fort.

Worship is about God and entertainment is about us. If we allow "entertaining" to mean "engaging," we welcome the dynamic to worship. If, however, "entertaining" means distraction or amusement, the focus of worship is in jeopardy. As worship becomes more entertaining in this sense, worship leaders must as well. During the years framed by Vatican II and the beginning of the twenty-first century we saw the titles of the leaders of worship's music move from *song leader,* to *minister of music,* to *minister of music and worship,* to *worship minister,* to titles such as *worship producer, pastor of celebration,* and *minister of magnification.* These titles, all still in use in various free-church congregations, can be seen as evidence of a developing understanding of worship. They also speak to the diversity of worship styles within the church. However, we must ask if that sequence of titles does not cast a shadow created by the bright light of show business. If the technology, the music, the talent, and the personalities are within reach, why not be as entertaining as the television? (This question will appear again in chapter seven.)

Worship must be engaging. To be worshipers, the congregation must be participants; they must engage heart and mind, spirit and truth. Worship, being a dialogue that God initiates, calls for a response that is not unlike engaging God in conversation. God initiates, we respond. Worship leaders are called upon to facilitate the response. Worship wars flared when the more energetic of the veterans of the front interpreted the term "worship leader" to mean the first person to enter the holy of holies. Veterans of the fort insisted that the temple veil had been torn in two from top to bottom, that God had come to us and is with us, that we no longer needed to "come into God's presence" from someplace outside of it in order to be close enough to worship God. "Remember, I am with you always, to the end of the age" (Matt 28:20b, NRSV). Something as deep in the soul as a Christian's understanding of where God is, is worth "going to war" over. Is not the presence of the Holy Spirit the presence of God? The doctrine of the Trinity is being challenged when someone who claims to have Jesus in his or her heart talks of entering the presence of God as an option. The fort had been invaded. Veterans of the front were declaring that Christian popular music or, at least, the music fashioned after it was necessary for worshipers to "enter the presence of God."

Worship is *acknowledging* God's presence in a special way by means of a focused and humbled heart. The dialogue initiated by the ever-present God transforms the worshiper. The more we think about this kind of acknowledging and engaging, the more the conventional understanding of entertaining leaves us. Yet, the music, meant first to be entertaining, remains.

Of course Christian popular music remains. It is the expression of many talented Christian musicians. It is the joy of many Christians who listen and celebrate the freedom and grace the music proclaims. It provides a welcomed alternative on the radio dial and the music store shelves. However, it is involved in a battle on two fronts: (1) Does it respond to or create its audience? and (2) What place does it have in corporate, congregational worship? In that environment, the two camps congregate for survival, nourishment, and encouragement.[5] Arenas and occasions for dialogue must be created. Christian popular music, better known as contemporary Christian music (CCM), and the leaders and educators of traditional church music must talk to each other. They must restore community. They are, after all, brothers and sisters in Christ, gifted and called by God for kingdom purposes.

So how did Christian popular music make its way into the fort? There were at least three paths of "infiltration."

The Music and the Church Soloist

In the free-church tradition, the musical testimony of a soloist from among the congregation (most often a member of the choir) has long been an honored element of worship. Here, a person with better than average vocal skills sings the personal songs of the faith that are perhaps beyond the skills of the congregation and better suited to one person's testimony than to the group expression of the choir. Often, the solos selected are from outside the congregational and choral repertories. The soloist is well known and respected within the congregation (though "guests"

---

[5] For an excellent description and evaluation of Christian popular music, see Charlie Peacock, *At the Cross Roads: An Insider's Look at the Past, Present, and Future of Contemporary Christian Music* (Nashville: Broadman and Holman, 1999).

are occasionally afforded the privilege). Here, the Christian popular or Contemporary Christian song finds its easiest entry into the
fort. A song unfamiliar to the congregation is received as a gift.
The soloist brings the congregation something new. Depending on
the soloist's skill, the rendition comes close or not so close to that
of the recorded version by the Christian artist.

Should the theology of the solo be somewhat questionable, as
is often the case with non-denominational popular songs, it is easier to excuse because it is, after all, a particular individual's personal testimony. This is challenged occasionally by the alert pastor
or minister of music, but often allowed to slip by. Should the
congregation or its representatives, the choir, sing the same questionable theology it would be another matter. The corporate
expression is a more significant declaration of the congregation's
doctrine.

For those who know the recorded version, the soloist's voice
and rendition are quietly compared to the way its supposed to be
done. The soloist is admired for knowing the song and for giving it
a humble try. The soloist is admired even more for bringing a bit
of the contemporary, the real world, into the staid and traditional
setting of worship. He or she is seen as something of an innovator
who has the courage to step outside of "the box." The singer of the
contemporary Christian solo was received by veterans of the fort
much like a missionary from some distant part of the front, home
to show their slides, home to explain how the Christian message is
expressed in another culture. One hears echoes of the incongruent
philosophy of "we'll send missionaries to them—we just don't
want them to join the church."

Through the testimony of the congregational soloist, the Christian popular songs found a place inside the fort. Though the word
"infiltration" was used earlier, "invitation," born of Christian hospi-
tality, is probably the better word.

After singing his or her solo, this trusted insider returned to the
choir loft or a pew in the sanctuary.

The Music and the Church Choir

It didn't take long for publishing companies to produce choral
arrangements of Christian popular songs that had made it into the
fort and survived. If the soloist could sing the popular song out on
the platform on Sunday morning, why couldn't he or she sing it

once returned to the choir loft to rejoin the adult choir? The minister of music, showing that his or her courage and awareness matched those of the soloist, purchased the SATB arrangements of the Christian artists' solos. It was soon evident that thirty average voices could not do what one exceptionally talented voice could do. Yet (we) the valiant Ministers of Music pressed on. For choir members who didn't know the songs, the new repertory was simply that . . . new and difficult. For the veterans of the fort seated in the pews, the music was simply unfamiliar. Much of it was tolerated. Often, the extent of the toleration was in direct ratio to the trust placed in the Minister of Music. Some of the Christian popular music sung by the choir, however, was quite well received by the congregation. It must be remembered that the choirs within the forts were made up of members of the church, many of whom were well respected and held responsible positions in other areas of congregational life and ministry. It was not unusual for the congregation to adapt their level of comfort to this music from the front.

As was mentioned in chapter two, the youth choir frequently was the choral entry point for music of the front. Indeed, youth choirs sang some of the chorally arranged Christian popular music. But, in this case, the difficulty of the music often caused the minister of music to by-pass the youth choir and turn immediately to the adult choir.

Now, Christian popular music had a larger voice and place in worship. The adult choir was/is a significant subset of the congregation. What about the congregation's song?

The Music and the Congregation

Though adult or sanctuary choirs can be useful in bringing new people into the church, most often they are populated by those who have emerged from the congregation. In addition to holding responsible positions throughout the church, choir members are friends and family members of the congregation. These are strong personal connections. There are musical connections as well.

For Southern Baptists the legendary link was *The Broadman Hymnal*, 1940. This hymnal, still in print (though its 1956 and 1975 Baptist hymnal successors are not), includes in its "Topical Index," a category labeled "Choir Selections." Thirty-seven songs are listed

there. Some of the songs listed are congregational hymns with
choir options presented by the inclusion of grace notes. Others,
however, are arrangements clearly designed for choir use only. We
have already mentioned the influence youth musicals had on the
Baptist Hymnal, 1975. In similar fashion, *The Baptist Hymnal,* 1991
reflects the congregations' love for the music of the popular Christian artists. Some of these songs moved directly from the concert
stage and recording to the hymnal, bypassing the choir loft. However, in many, perhaps most, cases, that congregational love for
songs from the Christian popular music repertory came after hearing, or was reinforced by the hearing, of the choir singing the choral arrangements. "We Shall Behold Him," "There is a Savior," and
"People Need the Lord" are examples. If accessibility was a factor
in bringing Christian popular song from recordings to the choir, it
certainly was when such song moved to the congregation. But the
congregation's musical ability was more carefully taken into
account. If these "hymns" were not accepted, it could not be on
the grounds of inaccessibility.

Songs of the front were firmly entrenched within the fort, baptized by immersion into the second most important book in free-
church worship, the hymnal. Fierce battles break out when the
war breaches the walls of the fort. The fort in the case of a denominational hymnal, however, is bigger than the local congregation.
Denominational hymnals, perhaps to a greater extent than non-
denominational hymnals, reflect what's happening in the congregations more than they initiate it. Where congregational song
repertory is a cause for war, the hymnal simply serves as a report
published by the war correspondents who served on the hymnal
development committee.

SIX

The Fastest Growing Churches—and Similar Reports

> *The power of persuasion lies not in human
> ingenuity and creativity, nor in techniques
> and methods, but in God's communication.*
>
> Douglas D. Webster[1]

The Church Growth Movement

It is not a bad thing to want local congregations to grow, but a good thing. We are to tell people the good news of Jesus. When, in response, people commit their lives to Christ, they should become members of a local community of Christ-followers for nurturing and spiritual growth. It is our hope that they will subsequently become authentic messengers of the good news. In many cases, it will have been such a community that nurtured the person toward faith in Jesus in the first place.

So why, then, would a chapter in a book about worship wars be dedicated to something as obviously proper as "church growth," something as agreeable as evangelism? In many circles, to question the church growth movement is to speak against evangelism, but neither this book nor its author speak against evangelism. However, I *am* to be numbered among those who believe that church growth as a defined and articulated goal, *superimposed on worship,* did and does contribute to America's worship wars. Turn ahead, if you must, to chapter nine and read my positive commentary on Sally Morgenthaler's excellent and important book *Worship Evangelism*. Neither church growth nor

---

[1] *Selling Jesus: What's Wrong with Marketing the Church* (Downers Grove, Ill.: InterVarsity, 1992), 16.

evangelism suffers when they wait for their impetus to come from uncluttered worship. Church growth and evangelism, like all else in the life and work of the church, are enlivened and energized by people who have left all else at the bottom of the mountain in order to worship God together.

Another risk in suggesting that the church growth movement might somehow be one of the contributors to worship wars is the implied suggestion that you are speaking against success. This was mentioned earlier in the opening pages of Part II. How can you argue with success? The question is meant to be rhetorical, a conversation stopper, an ace up the sleeve. However, it is *not* rhetorical.

The concept of "the *(fill in the number)* fastest growing churches in *(fill in the blank)*" was a popular subject and title for books and articles in the 1970s. The phrase often introduced pseudoscientific statistics in conferences and sermons. But the reports engendered hope and energy. They presented the possibility of regaining a momentum that had not been ours, perhaps, since the 1950s. There was hope that such focused enthusiasm and proven success could rescue our society. As strong as these motivations were, as much as the society needed the gospel, as strong as the "church growth" movement was—and to a degree still is—within two decades Kennon L. Callahan would write, "We have been preoccupied with whether our churches are growing; we should be preoccupied with whether our mission is dying."[2]

Often, the secrets of "the fastest growing churches" were identified and reduced to a list shorter than your grocery list. Why would any congregation choose not to follow the formula? Success was being offered free of charge. The fastest growing churches, now with significant "head starts," could be generous and further spread the gospel by spreading the formula. Small congregations were "not yet big." "Plateaued" churches were seen as unsuccessful, locked in an old paradigm, having unskilled leadership, or, in some way, gently punished by God for not being spiritual enough. "Plateau" was the first step down from church growth to church death. If churches were properly aligned with God and the culture, according to the general precepts of the church growth movement, they would grow. Of course, "growth" meant numbers. The church growth movement could produce statistics that

---

[2]Kennon L. Callahan, *Effective Church Leadership* (San Francisco: Harper Collins, 1990), 18–19.

proved that a plateaued church was like a baseball tossed straight up into the air. At its zenith (its plateau) the next movement was inevitably down.

One of the most effective pastors I have ever known retired thinking he had not accomplished much for the Lord. For most of his career, his congregation numbered one hundred or fewer. His was a "small church." His congregation had been featured in an article in one of their denominational periodicals because of the missions (new congregations) they had birthed, the uniqueness of some of their ministries, and the seminary student staff members they had "trained." But that article appeared before the church growth movement gained momentum. In church growth terms, his small church had failed. They had not become larger at the mother church address.

High on many of the "fastest growing churches" lists, often number two after "strong pastoral leadership" (read "CEO"), was a celebrative, energetic, or exciting worship style.[3] Who could resist? The changes could be made quickly and for all to see. The changes in worship were often incremental. To start first with the music was the common understanding. If that "works," you can stop there. If that didn't produce enough results, add technology for sight and sound enhancement. Casual dress was next. If more measures were needed, the pastor might consider making adjustments in sermon preparation and delivery. Remodeling of the sanctuary toward a less "churchy" environment was not uncommon. These measures were all in the context of worship. Changes in Bible study (Sunday School) and outreach methods could be employed, but were considered best attempted in new church starts.

Obviously, none of the measures listed above are, in and of themselves, necessarily wrong or destructive. The difficulties arose at the point of change management. Decisions were made by the pastor alone, or by the pastor and a small group of staff. Implementation was often immediate. The urgency of the church growth movement became the pastor's "war powers act." It is not surprising that "worship wars" erupted in these settings. With subtleties steamrolled, concerned congregants responded in the only ways left to them, sudden shouts and resistance or compliance.

---

[3] The word "exciting" became quite important in the church growth movement. It was not unusual to get something like the following greeting when phoning the office of a fully committed church growth congregation: "Good morning, Exciting Calvary."

Popular Demographics

In his book *Dining with the Devil,* Os Guinness argues that "the church-growth movement is vulnerable to contemporary conceit at two main points. The first is where it under-estimates the power of the present in its arguments—for example, in its reliance on futurism. . . . Church growth's second vulnerable point is the reverse—where it overestimates the power of the present in its arguments."[4]

It is not the fault of the facts when information is misapplied. Demographics, like any science, and futurists, like any thinkers, can be received in both constructive and destructive ways. Misapplication of good information can happen in at least two instances. It can happen when proper application of the information has produced all the good it can; yet it is called upon to stretch beyond its value. Another instance of misapplication is when successful application of information in one arena is taken as assurance that it can be juxtaposed into a totally different arena with equal and appropriate success.

One of the most influential demographers/futurists to appear in the second half of the twentieth century is George Barna. Founder and president of his own research group, his "Christian clients have included the Billy Graham Evangelistic Association, The Navigators, Focus on the Family, Campus Crusade for Christ, World Vision, Compassion International, CBN and numerous other organizations and churches."[5] One cannot help but notice the impressive group of para-church organizations that appear in a list that concludes with "and churches." People are people, facts are facts, and our society encompasses churched, para-churched, and non-churched people. George Barna and others of his profession scout the land on behalf of veterans of the front and the fort alike. In Barna's own words, "We are interested in that which is solid but flexible. The Christian faith, as promoted in our churches today, offers few of these traits."[6] But we must ask, "Do the studies that help para-church groups help local congregations in the same way?" Forgive the length of the following quote from the 1976

---

[4]Os Guinness, *Dining with the Devil* (Grand Rapids, Mich.: Baker, 1993), 80–81.
[5]George Barna, *The Frog in the Kettle: What Christians Need to Know About Life in the 21st Century* (Ventura, Calif.: Regal, 1990), back cover.
[6]Ibid., 119.

book *Your Church Can Grow: Seven Vital Signs of a Healthy Church,* but it is included because it documents the linkage between para-church organizations, local congregations and church growth. To be fair, I must point out that this quote is followed in subsequent pages by an admission that "a good celebration alone does not make for a healthy, growing church." However, the implication of the para-church experience and church growth is not diminished.

> Christian festivals and celebrations have been a long-standing tradition in American Christianity . . . although they have taken on different forms and names at different times. The great camp meetings of a century ago, Finney's revivals, Billy Graham's crusades, summer Bible conferences, Urbana missionary conventions—all these have operated basically as celebrations. They were and still are functional substitutes for the Jewish festivals. Christians love to go to them. They are a lot of fun!
>
> Some Sunday morning worship services in our churches are fun, too. Unfortunately, however, the Sunday morning service in many churches is more like a funeral than a festival. There is nothing unauthentic about that kind of worship service—true, committed Christians can and do get through to God under such circumstances. But it is not the kind of experiences that they are very enthusiastic in inviting their unconverted friends to. Why not admit it? It's no fun!
>
> This is probably one reason why many churches have remained small over the years . . . The problem could very well be that the churches are simply too small. Good celebrations need lots of people to make them fun and attractive.[7]

What does "para" mean? A quick look at the dictionary reveals some interesting definitions. The prefix does not mean "anti," but the definitions do include "beyond," "beside," "aside from," and "amiss." These indicate a relationship, even closeness, to the word that follows the hyphen, but we cannot escape the fact that "para" means something other than the central or core entity. Barna's statistics tell us about the values and habits of the kingdom of this world, not the kingdom of heaven. Can an over-reliance on statistics and demographic studies, produced largely for para-church ("aside from" the local congregation) organizations, and aimed toward evangelism, lead a congregation to "para-worship"?

---

[7] C. Peter Wagner, *Your Church Can Grow: Seven Vital Signs of a Healthy Church* (Ventura, Calif.: Regal, 1976), 112–13.

I define "para-worship" as the motions and emotions of worship without the context and responsibilities of community. Para-worship leaders do not have to know the members of the congregation/audience. They are not their ministers. Para-worship does not have to take multiple generations of worshippers into account. The audience at the rally/concert/gathering will not only be of like mind, they will probably all be of like age. If it is not like that at the beginning, it will become that way.

Para-worship is brought in from the outside, superimposed, not adopted. It is brought in from the outside while authentic worship wells up from within the soul of the congregation. Any who have proclaimed the word of God know the difference between preaching from your own pulpit in the context of your congregation and preaching one of those sermons as a guest in another setting. Something is missing. Truth isn't missing. Scripture isn't missing. What is missing? It is the authenticity of community that boils up out of the congregation. It is knowing the hearts and lives of the congregation. Preaching works here as an example because it is a part of worship. A few decades ago preaching was worship. Now music is worship. Both concepts are corrected when brought to the understanding that preaching is part of worship. Preaching that enriches, heals, and challenges with understanding rather than naiveté, with compassion rather than formula, can only come from one whose heart is the heart of the community; so, too, for all of worship. If it is imported without being adopted, if it is superimposed without community roots, it is "para" . . . not "anti," but other than. Worship leaders are tempted to import para-worship because it is seen as a shortcut toward a worthy goal. Someone else has done the homework, made the changes, read the demographics and re-aligned the methods. Someone else manufactured it; all we have to do is buy it. The easy road, the brightly lighted road, is not always the path we are to follow. Following Jesus often means leaning into a hill, taking steps that are illumined only one at a time. It is a paradox that while para-worship has a costly price tag, it costs us too little. Much of the resistance to imported and imposed para-worship comes from a spiritually innate, though unarticulated, understanding that a deep connection is missing, that what we are doing takes place somewhere above or outside of the soul.

Para-worship is the "flip-side" of what Sally Morgenthaler calls "nonworship" and it is not limited to a specific style. She reports "The nonworshiping churches I visited ran the gamut from those on the far end of the culturally relevant style spectrum to those that are stylistically conservative."[8] "Nonworship" differs from para worship in that it can be the shell of what once did, in fact, rise up from the soul of the congregation. "Nonworship," as coined and described by Morgenthaler, finds its influencing disconnect at the point of interaction with God, whereas para-worship's disconnect is at the point of interaction with the congregation. The results are same, "worship counterfeits."[9]

Local congregations have, in many cases, learned that sharing the same statistics with para-church organizations does not imply wisdom in sharing the same application. In an emergency, away from a hospital, brave and dedicated paramedics can communicate my vital signs to a hospital staff and give me first aid, even highly informed and sophisticated first aid, but I want a surgeon to perform the surgery. At the hospital, para-medics go no farther than the emergency room. Veterans of the front, in this case proponents of the "church growth" movement and demographics, often argue that "the world" is in a constant state of emergency and, therefore, local congregations should be "M.A.S.H." units. Veterans of the fort would not argue the intensity or urgency of the world's plight. Indeed, veterans of the fort who are committed to the church's continuation of Christ's mission know that "the interaction between the gospel and all human cultures is a dynamic one, and it always lies at the heart of what it means to be the church."[10] They would, however, argue that, in terms of our current metaphor, the sanctuary is not an emergency room.

Paul Duke reminds us "every sermon is addressed to traumatized people."[11] He's right. But even so, worship is not an emergency procedure for the dying. Worship is for the living God. Worship is an act of the believer and the believing soul is eternally alive, no matter how bruised or battered. No heroic measures are needed. Through worship, wounded believers are *nurtured* toward health and healing.

---

[8]Sally Morgenthaler, *Worship Evangelism* (Grand Rapids, Mich.: Zondervan, 1995), 50.

[9]Ibid., 51.

[10]Darrell L. Grueder, ed., *Missional Church: A Vision for the Sending of the Church in North America* (Grand Rapids, Mich.: Eerdmans, 1998), 14.

[11]David Nelson Duke and Paul D. Duke, *Anguish and the Word: Preaching That Touches Pain* (Macon, Ga.: Smyth & Helwys, 1992), 4.

Church growth and demographics are braided around the original strand, evangelism. The resulting rope is called "success." Colloquial wisdom knows what happens when one is given "enough rope." Yet, as stated earlier, one simply cannot argue with success. To do so is seen as un-American, un-motivated, un-Christian, and soft. Wars are ignited when religion, nationalism, and economics are mixed in one grail into one concoction that is drunk by those who are with us and refused by those who are against us. Worship wars are no different. When success is worshiped, war will result.

Good things happen. Good things come from work and honesty and commitment and unselfishness. Good things, however, can be tainted and spoiled when they are labeled "success" and, therefore, advertised and sold as the current best or only way. Success says, "Follow me," and we assume it to be the voice of Jesus. Young recruits in Marine Corps boot camp soon learn the voice of their drill instructor. They learn it so well that they are not distracted in the least by commands bellowed to another platoon by another drill instructor, even though the other recruits and D.I.'s are in the same organization, doing the same training, and will, someday, fight side by side. The Great Shepherd said, ". . . the sheep follow him because they know his voice" (John 10: 4b NRSV). They do not mistake the voice of success for the voice of Jesus. Jesus also said, "You cannot serve God and wealth" (Luke 16:13 NRSV). Is it a stretch to replace the word "wealth" with the word "success"?

Mega-churches

> For their hugeness they are often known, and often chagrined to be known as megachurches. Among the other labels one hears are full-service churches, seven-day-a-week churches, pastoral churches, apostolic churches, "new tribe" churches, new paradigm churches, seeker-sensitive churches, shopping-mall churches. . . . These very large and dynamic congregations may at the moment number no more that 400, but they are the *fastest-growing* [italics mine] ones in the country.[12]

It is easy to do bad math here: success is not be worshiped (2), mega-churches are successful (+2); therefore, megachurches must worship success (=5). Megachurches may or may not have fol-

---

[12] Charles Trueheart, "Welcome to the Next Church," *Atlantic Monthly* (August 1996): 38.

lowed the voice of success instead of the voice of Jesus. However, there is no doubt about which voice smaller churches are responding to when they use time, money, people, and worship to be mega-like rather than Christ-like.

Seldom does a small church (or a conference leader) look to a megachurch's retirement home high-rise, or their shopping mall food court and say, "Let's do that." Why? For one reason, only some of these unusual activities for a congregation may have actual ministerial value. They also may well be beyond the resources of the smaller congregation. However, it may be because we are quicker to look to the showplace (worship) than to the workplace (ministry) for our new investments of time and energy. We certainly are hesitant to follow the "successful" into the unknown place (innovation), even though

> He comes to us as One unknown, without a name, as of old, by the lakeside, He came to those who knew Him not. He speaks to us the same word: "Follow thou me!" and sets us to the tasks which He has to fulfill for our time. He commands, and to those who obey Him, whether they be wise or simple, He will reveal Himself in the toil, the conflicts, the sufferings which they shall pass through in His fellowship, and as an ineffable mystery, they shall learn in their own experience Who He is.[13]

If innovation was our response to the "success" of the megachurches instead of imitation, and if we were as drawn to the workplace and the unknown place as quickly as we are the showplace, worship might not be the scene of sudden and destructive warfare. War often starts when one party (nation, tribe, etc.) wants what another party has. They go to war for it, rather than going to work for it. In terms of worship we want their success, their contemporary sound, their casual approach and attire, their liberation. We "take it," through imitation and it is no more "ours" than if we had stolen it. We must be able to honestly own our worship. We can "own" (accept as ours) what Jesus gives us when we follow him. It will well up from within our community. There will be warfare, but it will be spiritual and against the powers of darkness, not verbal and emotional against one another.

Mega-churches are spectacular. They get to be church and exhibit the most sparkling of the world's "legal" indulgences at the

---

[13] Albert Schweitzer, *The Quest of the Historical Jesus* (New York: Macmillan, 1968), 403.

same time. What small, tired congregation wouldn't be attracted to the sight? But when the answer to "How can we get in on that?" leads to forced and shallow imitation, to "para-worship," the small congregation has adopted only the "legal indulgences," not an enriched experience of being church.

Being in Worship

Throughout the pages of this book, we have seen how aspects of the church's mission and other good concerns can be "other gods," can be distractions within worship. For just a moment, let's consider how these distractions work. Our time of worship has two "intensities" about it. One, worship is the deepest expression of our Christianity. Second, worship is often the most populated hour in the congregation's week. These two lenses of focus are known to all in the congregation, whether consciously or subconsciously. Therefore, members of the congregation will innately filter what issues may or may not be addressed appropriately in the worship hour. Each issue (distraction from worship) important enough to enter this arena will, of course, have its champions. This causes an immediate division of the congregation, for others in the congregation will deem the same issue "secondary." As has been stated earlier, worship unites, issues and agendas divide. The "high ground" of worship is to be desired, at times, fought for. The cycle takes us back to the important issues of evangelism and church growth (often a lofty euphemism for church survival). The thinking is that such important issues should benefit from the "high ground" of worship. This should be the arena. Here one's intensity and focus match the perceived importance of the issues. And quietly, but unmovingly, Jesus sits alongside surrounded by the echoes of "You shall have no other gods before me" and "Father, make them one, even as we are one."

The difference between doing something for God and being something because of God is slight, but significant. The being must come first. Doing must grow out of being, especially in the context of worship. What are we to be in worship? We are to be humble. We are the creatures coming before the Creator and chief among the assembled sinners. We are to be honest—no pretense, no pretending, hearts exposed in confession, nothing "para" in our hearts or actions. We come before God with nothing good to offer. We have tainted godly causes, found self-serving aspects in every ministry, betrayed in word, deed, or ignorance God's grace and call in our lives. It is difficult to champion a cause when there is nothing about us that is of championship character before the Almighty and Holy One. In true worship, we rejoice in God's victories and successes, God's strength, God's mercy, God's love. Our most righteous accomplishments, dreams, and ambitions are embarrassed before the One who created everything, including us and our salvation, and who knows our real heart. Can we shove God aside and call it worship? Can we dare to come into worship for the purpose of working on our projects? Do we think we can impress God with our work when we are to be bowing before God with our confession and praise? Who are we at the moment of worship? Are we workers coming back to the throne to report on *our* progress, coming to show God *our* innovative plans, displaying *our* interpretations of his commandments? We have nothing to offer God but broken-hearted confession, followed by whole-hearted praise and adoration, followed by well-intentioned, but half-hearted commitment, knowing full well that God knows our every heart and loves us still. Our prayers, songs, and sermons are the best we have. Clothed in the honesty of the individuals and the community we embody we become the gifts of children, presented to a gracious and loving parent.

If our worship is warfare, it is because we come to worship doing rather than being.

SEVEN

Television Church

*This is not a retelling of the
biblical narrative; it's the
recapitulation of prime time.*

Thomas G. Long[1]

Technology and Responsibility

If the technology, talent, music, and personalities are available, why shouldn't worship be as professional and entertaining as
the television? We first encountered this question in chapter five.
Let's look at the question more closely.

Television was only one of the technological advances that
raced through the last four decades of the twentieth century, but it
was an important segment because of its phenomenal influence on
society. The progress could be seen in both production techniques
and electronic capabilities. The technological leaps forward, while
not as rapid as those of the computer, were nearly quantum in
nature, and television soon leapt into the sanctuary.

What could be said and shown on TV changed along the
way but, thankfully, did not affect worship. However, keeping
the obviously objectionable and profane out of worship is not
enough. New technology should not be adopted into our worship,
or anywhere else for that matter, without considering the demands
of that technology and its effect on worship. The field of medicine
is a good and perhaps the first example. There, we discovered that
if new technology *could* keep the patient alive, it was somehow
automatically assumed that the patient *must* be kept alive. That, of
course, is not necessarily ethically or morally true. Technology is

[1]"Between Opposing Forces: Finding a 'Third Way' in Worship,"
Congregations 27:4 (July/August 2001): 8–11.

so closely attuned to science, and, during the modern era, science was so widely accepted as "the" truth, any related ethical questions were assumed to be answered or made passé. Transferring that line of thinking to television and worship, the thought process seemed, and seems, to be, if advances in television *can* be employed in worship they *must* be employed in worship. Again, this is not necessarily true.

Turning again to Charles Reich and his book *The Greening of America* (1970), we open to his chapter titled "It's Just Like Living." Writing about technology and the environmental crises, he made a statement that applies to our concerns. He wrote:

> We are guilty of a moral failure, that in our rush to acquire and grow, we have not paused to tend to deeper qualitative values; we have simply not assumed moral responsibility for how things are used— the ends to which new technology and systems are put.[2]

Veterans of the fort stopped short of accusing the veterans of the electronic front of "moral failure," but questions were certainly raised at the point of "deeper qualitative values." Lights, screens, television cameras, sound boards, and hand-held microphones found their way into the sanctuary and were seen by veterans of the fort as something more than new tools.

This story actually begins with radio, pre-dating this book's stated starting point, Vatican II. In their day, the more innovative congregations were those who broadcast their worship over the radio. Even though broadcasts of religious music and preaching were already being aired, broadcasting a congregation's worship service was an innovative idea. It moved the church beyond the walls of the fort at the speed of light. Veterans of the fort could feel the exhilaration of being a veteran of the front. The cost was minimal, often free. All that was required was that a congregation be willing to trade "Be still and know that I am God" (Ps. 46:10) for "Be still and loose your listeners" (ratings). Because radio had an audience, worship now had an audience. Meditation and silent prayer became "dead time." The radio audience's "dead time" was the exact moment in which worshipers were most "alive" to the presence of God. This blatant intrusion of the world's entertainment demands and accompanying technology was readily accepted. After all, filling silence with something for the radio

---

[2]Charles A. Reich, *The Greening of America* (New York: Random House, 1970), 158.

audience was more entertaining and comfortable for the congregation as well. Yet it would have been a tragic and indefensible oversight to ignore this opportunity to proclaim the gospel to the masses. Veterans of the fort and the front faced each other in a dynamic tension that had the potential for "warfare" or creative and positive solutions.

Perhaps the congregation had already been functioning as an audience, and radio simply brought the fact to light. Perhaps it was discovered that what served to attract and keep listeners also served to attract and keep attenders. But we must remember that "[the church] is not an audience positively inclined toward Jesus, but a company of committed individuals whose lives depend upon the truth that Jesus Christ is Lord. The church must not obscure this truth by transforming a congregation into an audience, transforming proclamation into performance or transforming worship into entertainment."[3]

When a congregation becomes an audience, the relationship between pastor and congregation is damaged. The sheep loose their shepherd. The sheep are not stolen, they do not wander off; they are, to an extent, abandoned by their shepherd. However gifted the pastor may be in the pulpit, he or she will not be able to sustain the pastoral role of preaching, the heart of preaching, if it is performance only. The congregation will detect the absence of "something." The pastor will not be fulfilled, nor energized by congregational rapport. There will be no ministry of the week to inform and enrich the preaching of the morning. Planning a show is not the same as preparing for worship. When the congregation is seen as an audience, the pastor will soon be working from personal talent alone. Exceptional and honed as the talent may be, preaching to an audience will deplete the pastor's spiritual, emotional, and physical energy. The pastor will know the sermon preparation process. He or she will remember the "timing" and "word-smithing" that have made the delivery so engaging in the past, but the poetry of it all will be gone. Entertaining an audience is not the same as engaging a congregation. This is true as well for musicians with worship leadership responsibilities. Still, properly understood and employed, crossing the air waves with the gospel was not unlike crossing the ocean waves in missionary endeavor.

---

[3] Douglas D. Webster, *Selling Jesus: What's Wrong with Marketing the Church* (Downers Grove, Ill.: InterVarsity, 1992), 16.

Worship's venture out of the fort via the airwaves turned something on that could not be turned off. As radio and movies paved the way for television, the big and little screens came to church. The middle-sized, stand-alone screen used to show missionary slides was relegated to the attic. The big screen was built in, hidden somewhere above and behind the pulpit. The little screen sent its cameras and lights to church like parents dropping their children off for Sunday School.

It would have been ridiculous for the church to ignore television. That would have been like Gutenberg refusing to print the Bible. In fact, it would have been impossible for the church to ignore television because the church is the people and people watch television.

> Perhaps nowhere is the intimate connection between religion and technology more manifest than in the United States, where an unrivaled popular enchantment with technological advance is matched by an equally earnest popular expectation of Jesus Christ's return. What has typically been ignored by most observers of these phenomena is that the two obsessions are often held by the same people.[4]

While it would have been impossible for the church to ignore television, it is interesting that worship was chosen for telecast. Why not Bible study on some early version of PBS? Catholic Bishop Fulton J. Sheen certainly captivated a TV audience with his teaching in the early days of television. For Baptists and other Protestants, small Bible study groups or Sunday School classes were known from the 1950s to the 1970s as the "outreach arm of the church." Wouldn't it have made sense for the "outreach arm" to reach out via television rather than televise the intimate family gathering known as worship? We return again to the possibility, if not probability, that worship had long been experienced as something akin to entertainment or performance. Even if that were not the case, bits and pieces of television's entertainment advances incorporated into the worship setting started the parishioners thinking about worship in ways they had not before. Of all the local church's functions, worship seemed the best suited for a viewing audience. In much of the free-church tradition, worship had long been evangelistic, often revivalistic. It was the most visual of the church's activities, it had a stage, seating arranged

---

[4] David F. Noble, *The Religion of Technology: The Divinity of Man and the Spirit of Invention* (New York: Knopf, 1997), 5.

toward the stage, hosts or "MC's," and plenty of people interested in precise starting and stopping times. Is it any wonder that worship overtook Bible study as the outreach arm of the church as the twentieth century neared its end?

We must remember, however, that television, itself, was not the enemy here. As was mentioned earlier, we have long known that each new technological advance brings with it new costs to be counted, new ethical questions to be considered.

> The link between religion and technology was not forged in the workshops and worship of the New World. Rather, the religious roots of modern technological enchantment extend a thousand years further back in the formation of Western consciousness, to the time when the useful arts first became implicated in the Christian project of redemption.[5]

A key phrase in this quote is "useful arts." We have almost lost sight of the sometimes subtle, but always significant, differences between science and technology and art and entertainment. During the second half of the twentieth century, entertainers began being referred to as artists. While it is sometimes true that artists are entertainers (Samuel Clemens, the great American writer, entertained thousands on his speaking tours), one wonders at the synonym status of the two words. The equality leads to the logic that if the high human endeavor of art reaches a larger audience as entertainment, the high human endeavor of worship can, thus should, as well. Television plays no favorites. Art, sport, education, worship—just about anything can be popularized, trivialized, or enhanced by television.

Technology that helps us on our way, but remains subservient to our understandings of worship *is* "useful," if not always "art." But when technology becomes the master, molding our theology into the shape of technology's capabilities, *we* are what's being "used," and "art" becomes propaganda, changing how we think, act, and respond. Interestingly, the same concern was addressed in para-church settings. Commenting on the televising of the Billy Graham Crusades, Martin Marty of the University of Chicago wrote in 1988, "While his association *uses* the medium *artfully* [both italics, mine], its camera picks up on the Graham who does what he did before it came to dominate. His cameras eavesdrop on evange-

---

[5] Ibid., 6.

listic rallies that would be the same without television."[6] In something of a Catholic version of a Billy Graham Crusade, Pope John
Paul II's 1979 visit to the United States included a televised open-
air celebration of the mass on the Boston Common. The mass was
celebrated (in a rainstorm) as it would have been indoors. The
telecast, however, was complete with commentators, much like a
baseball or football game. Yet, even though their play-by-play and
"color" commentary couldn't describe the taste of the eucharistic
elements, "the reverent viewer felt at one with the crowds at the
event and even sensed a feeling of grace as the pope extended his
blessings over the airways. Some viewers even phoned television
stations to be reassured that blessings received through their TV
screens were authentic."[7]

As usual, veterans of the front and veterans of the fort did not
agree on where the lines of technology and responsibility are to be
drawn in the context of a local congregation's worship. They did
seem to agree that issues of technology and responsibility were
deep enough to "go to war." The accusations began with the
familiar "going too slow" vs. "going too fast." In the highly sensi-
tized setting, the accusations grew through "behind the times" and
"cutting edge" to "entrenched" and "traitor," even "dead" and
"alive." Such conflicts are too easily and too quickly dismissed as
being between, in simple terms, those who can hook up their VCR
and those who can't. In fact, the deeper issue of the congregation
as an audience predates VCRs and all they symbolize. Whether or
not it was, or even could have been, articulated at the time, such
divisions and polarization, such wars, were born deep in the soul.
Somehow the warring parties sensed something profound to be
gained or something profound to be defended lest it be lost. As in
other disagreements, the heat of battle and sense of urgency left
little time for calm discussions and soul-searching. There was a
battle to be won, a battle with high stakes and consequences that
could not be reversed. The very immediacy and urgency that was
being experienced was a product of technology. Television must
air (now cable) its next show immediately, and the next episode of
the show just finished must be ready by next week. Admittedly,
the weekly worship services of a local congregation are somewhat

[6]Martin E. Marty, "Reflections on Graham by a Former Grump,"
Christianity Today 32:17 (November 18, 1988): 24.

[7]Gregor T. Goethals, *The TV Ritual: Worship at the Video Altar*
(Boston: Beacon, 1981), 129.

episodic as "the story" is told each week. But for the TV audience, re-runs are recognized and often suspect, if not resented. Next week's installment must be at least as engaging and entertaining as this week's—the more engaging and more entertaining the better. The sense of responsibility to the audience that drove the veterans of the front was challenged by the sense of responsibility to the congregation that drove the veterans of the fort. Worship was the arena.

Televangelism and Congregational Worship

Again, we find ourselves face to face with the question of the relationship between evangelism and worship. It is not a question that will go away, nor will it be diminished. The question's persistence speaks to its foundational nature. When the subject is war between sovereign states, debates in universities, national capitols, and barbershops seem always to return to economics as an underlying factor. When the subject is wars of an ethnic or tribal nature, religion and land are often placed at or near the core. In the case of America's worship wars, it seems that no matter what facet of the conflict we choose as a starting point, we eventually find the evangelism/worship question at or near the base. While oversimplifications are dangerous, identifying the crux of where and why the first rounds were fired may help us learn the hard lessons of this "war." The evangelism/worship question is certainly one of the major initial causes.

That having been said, we must be careful not to overstate the influence *televangelists* had on local congregational *worship* and its wars. How they affected preachers and other worship leaders and how they affected congregations cannot be assumed to be identical in substance or weight. Further, there are wide demographic gaps between the people who are attracted to televangelists and those who are put off by them, with very few in between. Even so, the "TV preachers" and their shows must be considered if we are to attempt a full-orbed study of the television church's contributions to America's worship wars. To be sure, "instead of driving people away from the church, televangelism is changing their very conception of the church and its functions."[8]

---

[8] Quentin J. Schultze, *Televangelism and American Culture: The Business of Popular Religion* (Grand Rapids, Mich.: Baker, 1991), 205.

In these pages, "televangelist" does not refer to those evangelists such as Billy Graham whose crusades were/are televised, but as established earlier, who do little if anything differently than they would if the event were not televised. Neither does it include the pastors of local congregations who televise their worship services within a relatively small viewing area. Here "televangelist" is used to describe those whose "ministries" exist for the television audience. They may stand behind a pulpit, sit behind the talk-show host's desk, skip across a stage, or, in some cases, sit on what can only be described as thrones. Though most often religious conservatives, they know full well that "the need to attract large audiences is one reason for avoiding doctrinal detail, [and that] audience expectations of stimulation move *producers* [italics mine] in the same direction."[9] There were, of course, exceptions to the avoidance of doctrinal details. The exceptions appeared most frequently in the televised existing worship services of congregations that freely used their denominational affiliation in the name of their church and/or program title. While doctrinal details may not have been avoided in these local instances, the scope of doctrines addressed was often narrow.

In the early days, televangelists saw their role as introductory, presenting the essentials for salvation, and encouraging the viewers to join local congregations for details, doctrine, and discipleship. However, few viewers did so. In fact, most viewers of religious television were already church members or committed non-members. The message of "joining" may have been lost on the viewers, but, in many cases, the model of "introductory" preaching and worship was not. As the years progressed and the televangelists became more focused on television and its revenue than on evangelism and supplementing the church, worship was increasingly used to describe the contents of the broadcasts. The shows were professional, expensive, opulent, and apparently successful on the world's playing field, but in the name of Jesus. The forces and fortresses of the devil seemed to diminish with each broadcast. Televangelist broadcasting teams seemed to be doing what local congregations were too poor, too slow, or too stodgy to

---

[9]Steve Bruce, *Pray TV: Televangelism in America* (New York: Routledge, Chapman and Hall, 1990), 70. Although mentioned earlier in this book, it must be mentioned again here, that a growing number of contemporary churches, near the end of the twentieth century, began changing the titles of their "Ministers of Music" to "Worship Producers."

do. It was not a stretch to think that if the televangelists had figured out how to save the world, maybe they had figured out how
to rescue the church at the same time. If worship in the local sanctuary could look and sound like the "worship" on the televangelists' sets, maybe those congregations could win their towns as fast
as the televangelists were winning the world. One of the problems
was, of course, that the televangelists had no live and present congregation. They had camera operators and other stagehands, perhaps a small studio audience, but no congregation to shape and
season and join the worship. Piles of mailed-in prayer requests
seemed to be evidence of a caring congregation, but they were,
in fact, evidence only of a needy audience. More recently, of
course, this has changed. Many televangelists interact with a
live congregation/audience in the studio. One hesitates, nonetheless, to use the word "congregation" when the program takes place
in a studio.

Ignoring the Congregation

The following thoughts are offered with the full knowledge
that in worship, God is the audience. Søren Kirkegaard, the nine-
teenth-century theologian, provided us a great service with that
reminder, even though his audience, actors, and prompters metaphor is open to some debate.[10] We move on.

Take the irresponsible engagement of technology that, among
other things, turns a congregation into an audience, and add the
televangelist's focus on increasing his audience, and you have a
mixture that produces the phenomenon of fort-to-fort competition.
This competition can create a focus that ignores or uses the congregation. Although television seems limitless in its possibilities,
there is heavy competition for the viewing audience, for "market
share." Because a relatively small percentage of the viewing public
watches religious programming, there is a need to work at attract-
ing and keeping an audience. This mind-set and urgency are inten-
sified for pastors of local congregations who focus first and
foremost on the television aspect of their ministry or the television
likeness of their worship.

---

[10] Søren Kierkegaard, *Purity of Heart Is to Will One Thing* (New York:
Harper, 1938), 160–66.

When the viewing audience is the focal point of the morning's worship experience instead of the attending congregation, the people in the pews play a different role. With only a few differences, the congregation becomes for the TV audience what the choir is to the congregation. When the people in the pews are, indeed, the congregation, the pastor has his or her back to the choir. The choir knows they are technically a part of the congregation and they understand the positioning, but while the people in the pews see the pastor's face, the people in the choir loft see the pastor's back. The choir knows they have an important part to play in the morning's event and they gladly participate, even benefit from their participation, but they are set apart. The choir exists to enhance the congregation's worship experience. Large, attentive choirs are seen as an encouragement to the congregation.

When, on the other hand, the TV audience is the primary focus of the morning's worship experience, the people in the *pew* take on a supporting role. They are there, they hear what's being said and sung, they participate, but, though they see the pastor's face, they, in effect, do not have the pastor's eye. The camera, wherever the pastor may be looking, has his or her attention. The pastor, with all good intentions, is overlooking the congregation.

As with the choir loft, so with the pews: the fuller the better. No one wants to sit out in the congregation and stare at empty choir chairs. No one watching on television wants the camera to pan across empty pews. *Audience impact*-related questions about empty chairs and pews or how they might be filled are easily answered in *congregational* terms. When more people are present, it follows that more people are worshiping. We need more people present for television, so let's find ways of getting more people present for worship. At one level, the solution or argument is beyond question. At another level, however, getting bodies in the empty seats, whatever it takes, for the sake of television, is the goal.

An example of ignoring the congregation for the sake of the TV audience can be seen in the church that had a problem with empty chairs in the choir loft. The large church had a choir loft that would seat some 300 singers. The Sunday morning worship services were televised. When choir participation leveled out between 200 and 250, vacant seats glared behind the pastor on the TV screen. The solution? Make an audiotape of the choir during the Wednesday night rehearsal. Then, on Sunday morning, assign adult Bible study classes, on a rotating basis, to sit, robed and with music-folder in hand, in the empty choir chairs. These extras could turn pages when the real choir members did and mouth the words. The audiotape from Wednesday night's rehearsal could be "stacked" on top of the real choir's singing, giving a vocal presence to the stand-in choir members' participation on Sunday morning. While we must give room for possible "urban-legend" enhancements of the actual event, this example grows out of the practice of an actual congregation. The creativity and ingenuity are to be commended. But, what are the people in the pews supposed to think about worshiping in truth, about how they are valued, about the validity of the worship experience? Such situations and lesser ones they might spawn in "want-to-be" or "competing" congregations are matters that ignored veterans of the fort would go to war over.

In other churches, the desire to put an attractive product on the TV screen has resulted in programming several attractions at the same time. Collecting the offering is an important part of worship. It is a means of involvement that both facilitates participation by the congregation in and through sacrifice and thanksgiving and meets the very practical financial responsibilities of that local body of Christ-followers. It is a time that should receive the focus of deep spiritual significance, humbly giving back to God a portion of what God has given to us. However, it doesn't play well on television. It's boring and sends the message that church is about money. So, how can that be corrected for the viewing audience? The answer? While taking the offering, have a soloist singing on the platform and have several people being baptized (immersion) in the pool behind and slightly above the choir loft. Now the multiple cameras have multiple points of interest. The producer can work with this. Where is the congregation?

More than once when hearing these examples in class, seminary students have asked me if I have made them up. My sad answer is that there is no need to make up such stories. Fact is stranger than fiction.

In still another instance, I was a part of a large number of people who were visiting a church in a city where a church music and worship conference was taking place. It was Sunday morning, so we decided to worship with this well-known congregation. Their worship service was televised. The members of the congregation and we visitors filled the sanctuary to overflowing. We were informed, before the service began, that, although the service was being televised live, there would be no extra or unusual accom-

modations for the viewing audience. *However,* we were also
instructed that when, in the service, visitors were asked to stand, it
would be appreciated if those of us who were in town for the conference would remain seated. The invitation to stand would be
only for those visitors who were residents of the town. Expecting
some sort of registration card to be distributed to those who would
stand, I felt the request was reasonable. But, there were no cards
distributed; registration of visitors was accomplished by means of
a card in the worship bulletin. Among the reasons that remained
was the haunting one that with the rest of us remaining seated, the
size of the local congregation would appear larger on screen. How
did the congregation feel?

On another occasion I was attending worship as a visitor with
a friend who was a member of the congregation. It was a large
church. As the choir entered I noticed two men in choir robes who
did not follow the others into the choir loft. Instead, they took
chairs on either side of the platform on which the pastor and other
worship leaders were seated. I watched to see what form their
worship leadership would take. As the worship service proceeded,
these two men only stood or sat with the flow of the liturgy, nothing more. I asked the friend what their function was. "They are
bodyguards," he said. "A while back some lunatic pulled a gun
and threatened to kill the pastor, right in the middle of church.
Guess he wanted air time on TV." The presence of the television
cameras was very much a part of the explanation. It is difficult to
argue with the logic of hiring bodyguards and making their presence known after such a frightening experience. However, that
episode heightened my awareness, and I began to hear accounts
of other pastors in other large churches with televised worship services also employing bodyguards. The television made them stars
and stars often attract "crazies," thus the bodyguards. I have been
around very few people who have had bodyguards. I have seen
one president in person and one governor. Their bodyguards were
expected and obvious. On television I have seen presidents and
college football coaches with bodyguards. In those cases, I understand the presence of the Secret Service agents and smile at the
presence of the State Troopers. I have had only one friend who felt
it necessary to employ bodyguards. Because of my job changes
and related relocations, I have lost touch with him. But our short
acquaintance could fairly be called a friendship. He would call
me to go to lunch with him, and I enjoyed each occasion. But on
each occasion bodyguards, in another car, seated at another table,

accompanied us. Though we never discussed it, I always felt like he was free to approach me, but that I needed to be cautious in approaching him. That was probably an exaggeration of the situation on my part, but it was there. How are the people in the pew supposed to feel when the pastor has bodyguards? They may well understand the safety issues, but they may also feel ignored— unless they pose a threat.

Do these examples call for us to turn off the spotlights and unplug the cameras? No. In fact, television and other technologies call for us to think more deeply and clearly about what we are doing in worship. When a new technology presents itself and we consider whether or not to use it in advancing the gospel, we are forced to revisit our philosophy and theology of worship, of evangelism, and of the two in contrast and concert. That is a good thing.

Worship wars are engendered, in part, by congregants who feel ignored or used. They will not tolerate being ignored or used as props for the benefit of television's viewing audience. Interestingly, while this is true of all veterans of the fort, it is especially true of the younger adults among them. Worship lies deep at the core of the soul, the very depth where the realities of war are processed.

EIGHT

The Language of Worship

*In time of war, language always
dwindles, vocabulary is lost.*

Madeleine L'Engle[1]

How important is our vocabulary? How deep in our being is
our language? A vocabulary change is a "sea change." It is a shifting of the continental plates on which our particular "world" rests.
The vocabulary and language of our youth and home, our education and vocation; these mark milestones in our development.
They speak of the path behind us. They speak of what we per-
ceive the path to be before us. Our vocabulary indicates the direction of our aspirations. The vocabulary and language of our
worship is no less significant.

There is a difference between vocabulary and language. One
can know a few words of the vocabulary of a foreign language
and know nothing of the language itself. The same holds true for
one's native tongue. I do not know all the words, let alone all the
definitions of all the words, in the vocabulary of English. However, I am sensitive to the power of the subtleties and nuances of
the English language and am unsettled at a deep level when
my vocabulary environment changes. As discussed earlier, vocabulary changes can be used as weapons or wedges. Language
changes speak of the soul of an environment, organization, or
movement. Vocabulary changes speak of the soul and intent of
those who have the positions and influence to make such
changes.

---

[1] *Walking on Water: Reflections on Faith and Art* (Wheaton, Ill.:
Harold Shaw, 1972), 41.

Vocabulary

Perhaps the most significant vocabulary change of America's worship wars was the change from "congregation" to "audience." Congregations did not rename themselves, their worship leaders renamed them, almost unconsciously. Audiences expect to be entertained in some way. They pay their money to see the show. Audiences are self-appointed critics. If the show does not please them, they attend only once, put pressure on the performers, or, with advance warning by word of mouth or professional critics, they don't come at all. They are not expected to be involved in the show except for what laughter or tears the performance can evoke. Audiences applaud—something, by the way, that veterans of the front love for its contemporary "amen" and veterans of the fort hate for its perceived cheapening of worship.

A congregation is a community, caring for each other, not only during the hour of worship, but throughout the week and in the comings and goings of life. An audience is a collection of strangers who may feel a momentary kinship in a laugh or cry, but nothing deeper or longer lasting than that. Congregations give of themselves while audiences keep to themselves, even in the midst of a crowd. Anonymity, not community, is the desire of an audience. Audiences are ready to leave as soon as the performance is finished, if not before. Congregations linger and visit and, when they do leave, they leave toward a purpose. Audiences watch or listen, congregations participate.

A full "house" means something different when referring to an audience than it does when referring to a congregation. The difference shows up in motivation and methods employed to fill the house and create anticipation. When the congregation changes to the audience, the physical focal point or source of activity moves from the pews to the "stage." The implications there need no commentary.

There were other vocabulary changes. The "mission field" within the United States became the "market place." Potential "converts" became a particular church's "market share." "Members" became "customers." Methods of "sharing" the gospel became "packaging." Indeed, the liturgy or order of worship began to contain "packages" of songs, Bible readings, and prayers. These words and the attitude shifts they reveal were used, often introduced or "baptized" in church growth conferences and books as well as in discussions (positive discussions) of changes in worship styles and congregational song repertory. In the eyes of the veterans of the fort, the veterans of the front had made worship a product to be packaged, sold, and exported. Worship was no longer a gift to be offered by the congregation to God. Worship often belonged to "seekers," no longer to a congregation happy to share the experience with "visitors."

The vocabulary shift from visitor to seeker seemed a step in the right direction, even for veterans of the fort. Seekers were first and foremost, the "un-churched" who were *seeking* Jesus. In its practical application, however, the word also included those who had drifted away from church or who were dissatisfied with their former congregation. In the thinking of veterans of the fort, these two groups of "unchurched" should not have to be wooed. Though they would be accepted if they chose to join, they should know better and simply grow up. Why should veterans of the fort have to change their ways for the sake of deserters? Every new word used in the context of worship was a reminder of the concessions being made, a hint that maybe the very language of Zion was shifting. For veterans of the front, the vocabulary concessions were merely the new, foreign language that needed to be learned in order to be effective missionaries.

Changes, some referred to already, in the titles of the worship leaders were also quite significant. Ministers of Music, Ministers of Music and Worship, and Associate Pastors who had worked their way up from Song Leader became Worship Producers, Ministers of Magnification, and Celebration Pastors. Could leaders with such new titles be expected to lead in the same old ways? Did the drop of "minister" from staff titles mean dropping the activity and relationship of ministry as well? "Ministry" seemed, in the new vocabulary, to be moving from among the lives of the congregation during the week to simply worship leadership from the platform on Sunday morning or Saturday night. Wouldn't changing the title "minister" to "producer," cause the members of the congregation to became supporting cast at best, perhaps only a part of the crowd scene? This is not even the "congregation as players" that Kirkegaard envisioned. Veterans of the fort, though often happy to see some sign of freshness in their worship, nonetheless felt slight tremblings beneath their feet and questions that, if asked, sounded like resistance. The deep rumble, felt across cities, states, and national conventions, was unsettling. Veterans of the front focused on the fact that "Minister of Magnification" or "Celebration Pastor" redefined worship, not the role of the leader. The differences seem easily resolved from their vantage point. But, in fact, the differences were a bit foreboding, resulting in some defensive posturing.

Language

Three major subsets of the larger subject of language became issues during the worship wars: archaic language, inclusive language, and militaristic language. Changes in these particular linguistics appeared in hymnals and translations of the Bible.

The archaic language issues were the move from "King James" English, especially (though not limited to) pronouns, to the language of the newspaper. Archaic imagery was also an issue. Inclusive language issues involved gender-specific references God and gender in general references to people. Militaristic language issues collided at the point of well-known references to spiritual warfare and the possible unintentional promotion of armed combat. Often, changes related to these separate language issues appeared simultaneously in a given context.

While "hath," "hast," and "eth- suffixes" might not have been missed, many veterans of the fort considered "Thee," "Thy," and "Thou" to be more reverent and respectful than "You" and "Your," as more appropriate worship language.[2] Veterans of the front, on the other hand, considered the words, pronouns included, to be from a former, if not foreign, language. The clashes between the two positions occurred on a philosophical level and in actual practice. Worship services where members of both camps were in attendance often contained this somewhat macaronic choral and congregational music, Scripture reading, and prayers.

A number of new "versions" of Scripture (that is to say, other than the King James Version) came into being during the 1960s and 1970s for the purpose of producing fresh translations from the ancient languages, fresh for their modern language designed to aid in understanding and application, fresh for their more recent and informed language study, or both. Two of the new versions had

---

[2] Readers are encouraged to see Michael Rathke's article, "An Apology for the Preservation of Archaic Language in Hymnody," in *The American Organist* 35:9 (September 2001): 64–68, its text and endnotes, for discussion from the "fort" on this issue.

great impact on what worshipers in America considered the proper "level" of English for the Bible. The very existence of these versions forced the question of whether a type of language acceptable for private worship was necessarily appropriate for corporate worship as well. The first of these more accessible versions was the paperback *Good News for Modern Man: The New Testament in Today's English Version* (1966)[3]—paperback! To some veterans of the fort paperback meant cheap and temporary. The other, one of the most popular and, at the same time, controversial, was *The Living Bible: Paraphrased* (1971).[4] It had actually been introduced a portion at a time beginning with *Living Letters,* 1962.[5] Veterans of the fort did not trust language changes to remain at the surface, especially in a Bible that admitted to being a paraphrase. New language meant new translation and new translation ran the risk of adjusted theology, something many people felt to be akin to blasphemy. For many who had grown up with the King James Version, this was the first time they had encountered the possibility of doctrinally-tempered preferences in word choices during the translation process. The joy that many felt over the freshness of new translations ran as high as the fear it engendered in others.

Reading from the Bibles the congregation brought with them could no longer facilitate a satisfying corporate reading of Scripture. There were too many translations with too many degrees of language modernization. The differing pronouns and sentence structure clashed like swords. The solution was either to limit Scripture reading to one person at a time or provide "pew Bibles." In the thinking of veterans of the front, pew Bibles constituted common ground. Page numbers could be announced for non-embarrassing ease in finding the passages. But what version should be selected? Also, it was often argued, pew Bibles are not personal. For some veterans of the fort, they symbolized a gap or separation between home and church connections with Scripture.

Changes in the wording of hymns did not go unnoticed either, nor were they accepted without thought and discussion. Some hymns are embedded as deeply as Scripture in the hearts of worshipers. When, in 1987, a committee was selected, assembled

---

[3] *Good News for Modern Man: The New Testament in Today's English Version* (American Bible Society, 1966).

[4] *The Living Bible: Paraphrased* (Wheaton, Ill.: Tyndale, 1971).

[5] *Living Letters* (Wheaton, Ill.: Tyndale, 1962).

as representatives of the people of the Southern Baptist Convention, and given the task of compiling *The Baptist Hymnal,* 1991, Dr. Wesley L. Forbis, Director of the Church Music Department of the Baptist Sunday School Board, had already given considerable thought to language issues. The Southern Baptist Convention was in theo-political turmoil. Many doubted whether a representative group of Southern Baptists (some 100) could gather in the same room and compile one hymnal. Several had advocated two or even three hymnals to accommodate disagreements over worship styles and theology. The decision was made to compile one book. It was the right decision and perhaps the last project for which Southern Baptists rose above political issues to *cooperate* (one of the SBC's most precious vocabulary and language concepts). Language was one of the points at which the committee's fragile peace and cooperative spirit was vulnerable. If over-emphasized or under-emphasized, the imbalance would have been misinterpreted as a theo-*political* statement. Therefore, the very first pages of the manual prepared for members of the hymnal committee contained a "Position Statement" prepared by Forbis and designed to set needed parameters. Portions of that statement are included here:

> No new texts will be included which contradict the affirmation of every believer as priest and participant in the mission of the church.
>
> To impose this guideline [above] on the more frequently sung traditional texts could (1) violate the historical context in which they were written, (2) distort our Christian heritage, and (3) impose forced and artificial poetic structure. Further, some of the classic texts are so familiar, so intimately bound to the spiritual life of the believer, and so firmly established in our worship practices that they are viewed as including all humankind: "There is neither Jew nor Greek, there is neither slave nor free, there is neither male nor female, for you are all one in Christ Jesus." [Galatians 3:28] Such texts, many of which are staples of congregational singing, provide their own historical testimony.
>
> Nevertheless, the committee may wish to recommend textual changes in those less familiar and frequently used hymns whose words or phrases are so outmoded that the original doctrinal meaning has been obscured or elitism or exclusivity implied.
>
> Inasmuch as the SBC is a cooperative body comprising many cultures, ethnic groups and worship practices, texts and music will, then, reflect the musical styles of the Convention body.

To fulfill this demand, hymns (text/music) will be selected from (a) all major historical periods, (b) various mission fields, as well as (c) the contemporary era.[6]

In the case of Southern Baptist hymnals, changes first came in small, manageable portions. For instance the move from the 1940 *Broadman Hymnal* to the 1956 *Baptist Hymnal* saw the dropping of some hymns and the addition of others, a process common in the development of all new hymnals. Without that, the next hymnal would not be new. Such changes, however, because they are anticipated, usually only generate discussions of opinion and preference. In this particular case, though, the change of one phrase in one hymn became a much discussed feature of the Convention's new (1956) hymnal. In Isaac Watts' "Alas, and did my Saviour bleed," the 1940 *Broadman Hymnal* included, in stanza one, the phrase "For such a worm as I." In the 1956 *Baptist Hymnal* the phrase was changed to "For sinners such as I." Here the discussions went deeper than opinion and preference. The motivation and theological significance of this change were discussed and debated for some time. This seemingly small word change in the midst of a new book was, somehow, as significant as the entire body of hymns that had been dropped or added. Why? The answer lies in the perception, even if subconscious, of where the line is drawn between vocabulary and language changes. An example of a similar change that, while annoying to some, remained at the level of vocabulary only, occurred in the next step in the development of Southern Baptist hymnals: the move from the *Baptist Hymnal,* 1956 to the *Baptist Hymnal,* 1975.

The *Baptist Hymnal,* 1956 contained a number of "new" hymns. One that was new to Southern Baptists was, interestingly enough, Fanny Crosby's (1820–1915) "To God Be the Glory," set by Baptist (not Southern) composer, William H. Doane (1832–1915). It quickly became a favorite of Southern Baptist congregations. Its third stanza contained the word "transport" used in a way that seemed, perhaps, a bit awkward, but was contained in a hymn that was otherwise quite satisfying. Its immediate context was the

---

[6]Wesley L. Forbis, "Position Statement" from unpublished *Manual: Hymnal Committees* in the possession of this author, pp. 1–3. For additional insight into the language issues related to the development of *The Baptist Hymnal,* 1991, see Wesley L. Forbis, "Currents and Cross-Currents Impacting Hymnal Formation: The New Baptist Hymnal, Issues and Answers," *Review & Expositor* 87:1 (Winter 1990): 75–88.

line, "But purer, and higher, and greater will be our wonder, our *transport,* when Jesus we see." Webster's second definition of "transport" as a noun is "rapture."[7] In the 1975 *Baptist Hymnal,* "transport" had been changed to "victory". Although somewhat in keeping with the original intent and definition, of "transport" (happiness or joy), one might wonder why "victory" was chosen as the substitute word rather than the word/definition "rapture." Fanny Crosby certainly used the word more than once in her hymns and gospel songs. In fact, the word "rapture" appears in four of her twelve gospel hymns in the 1975 *Baptist Hymnal.* The other three are "Blesssed Assurance, Jesus is Mine," "He Hideth My Soul," and "Redeemed, How I Love to Proclaim It." In each instance, "rapture" is used as an expression of emotion, not as an eschatological reference. Perhaps the difficulty of finding a two-syllable word for "joy" or "happiness" was the deciding factor. But, the new word that *was* chosen is a three-syllable word that had to be printed and sung as "vict'ry" to accommodate the meter. Something more than current usage had been adjusted. The new word was something of a commentary on the word it replaced. The change was noted as worshipers stumbled over a mixture of transports and victories for a time until the "new" word was anticipated as the third stanza approached. But, unlike the "worm" change experienced one hymnal earlier, it was received as a surface matter that elicited only smiles, not concern.

It should be noted that the word "rapture*d*" appeared in the refrain of Fanny Crosby's gospel song, "Jesus, Keep Me Near the Cross" in both the *Broadman Hymnal* (1940) and the 1956 *Baptist Hymnal.* Yet, in the1975 *Baptist Hymnal,* the word was changed to "ransom*ed*." The context here *is* one of eschatology, open to theological discussions of being "ransomed" before being "raptured." Like "transport" and "victory" mentioned earlier, "raptured" and "ransomed" bumped into each other in worship for only a few years and, evidently, without deep concern.

It was the *Lutheran Book of Worship,* 1978 [the *LBW*] that put American Christianity on notice that the language of worship, not just its vocabulary, was undergoing a change. Beginning in Lutheranism's subsets, news quickly spread across denominational lines that the Lutherans had taken great liberties with the language of hymns. Their bold steps had, perhaps, overstepped

---

[7]Victoria Neufeldt, ed., *Webster's New World Dictionary* (New York: Pocket Books, 1990).

the boundaries of good taste and historical integrity. In the "Introduction" to the *LBW,* the unnamed editor(s) wrote that "An examination of the contents will reveal the several goals toward which the Commission worked in liturgy . . . to bring the language of prayer and praise into conformity with the best current usage."[8] The breadth of support for the changes can be seen in the following paragraph from the same "Introduction":

> Through participation in groups such as the Consultation on Common Texts, the Consultation on Ecumenical Hymnody, and the International Consultation on English Texts, the Inter-Lutheran Commission on Worship has done its work in concert with other English-speaking churches. Through the Lutheran World Federation, contact has been maintained with other Lutheran churches of the world.[9]

What were these changes that caused such widespread notice, discussion, and concern? A comparison of selected hymns included in both the 1958 *Service Book and Hymnal*[10] and the 1978 *Lutheran Book of Worship* will serve as representative examples. Johannes Olearius' (1611–1684) hymn "Comfort, comfort ye, my people" appears in the 1958 book (hymn 12) with his title (translated by Catherine Winkworth, 1829–1878) and stanza two as follows:

> For the herald's voice is crying
> in the desert far and near,
> bidding all men to repentance,
> since the kingdom now is here.
>
> O, that warning cry obey!
> Now prepare for God a way;
> let the valleys rise to meet him,
> and the hills bow down to greet him.

In the 1978 book, the title was changed to "Comfort, Comfort Now My People" (hymn 29) and stanza two was changed to read:

> For the herald's voice is crying
> in the desert far and near,
> *calling us to true repentance,*
> since the Kingdom now is here.

---

[8] *Lutheran Book of Worship* (Minneapolis: Augsburg and Philadelphia: Board of Publication, Lutheran Church in America, 1978), 8.

[9] Ibid.

[10] *Service Book and Hymnal* (Minneapolis: Augsburg and Philadelphia: Board of Publication, 1958).

Oh, that warning cry obey!
Now prepare for God a way!
Let the valleys rise to meet him,
and the hills bow down to greet him!

Italics highlight the change of line three that facilitates the word change from "men" to "us." These changes were not to bring archaic language into contemporary vocabulary, as were some that we will see later. These changes were about inclusive language. While many people understood the clearer language sought in such changes, others saw only the issue of "women's liberation."

The medieval Latin carol translated by John Mason Neale (1818–1866), "Good Christian men, rejoice" (1958, numbered 39), is titled "Good Christian friends, rejoice" in the 1978 book. Again we go to the second stanza for comparison. In 1958, the second stanza was worded:

Good Christian men, rejoice
with heart, and soul, and voice;
now ye hear of endless bliss:
Jesus Christ was born for this!
He hath ope'd the heavenly door,
and man is blessed evermore.
Christ was born for this!

In the 1978 book the stanza is as follows:

Good Christian *friends,* rejoice
with heart and soul and voice;
now ye hear of endless bliss:
Jesus Christ was born for this!
He has *opened* heaven's door,
and *we are blest* for evermore.
Christ was born for this!

The italics point out changes made within the context of two issues here (one wonders why the archaic "ye" was left intact). First, the word "friends" and the phrase "we are" are obviously made for reasons of inclusiveness. The words "opened" and "blest" appear for the purpose of complete spelling and modern option, respectively. But here the title, more so than with "Comfort, comfort now my people," advertises the inclusive changes. It could also be argued that "Good Christian men, rejoice" is also more deeply imbedded in the "spiritual memory banks" of the people. The change was open to accusations of being a bit more intrusive. Nearly twenty years later, these changes seem natural. They were confined to references to people, not God. But, in the mid-seventies, such manipulation seemed to be capitulation. Social issues, some of which would later be given the derogatory label "political correctness," seemed to matter more, some thought, to editors than did proper, traditional worship.

"Lo, how a Rose e'er blooming," numbered 38 in the 1958 book, appears as "Lo, how a rose *is growing*" in the 1978 *Lutheran Book of Worship* (numbered 58). By this time, anthem settings had appeared that brought "e'er" up to date as "is." However, "blooming" had stayed in common usage. Here we turn to the first and second stanzas for our comparisons. In 1958 Lutheran congregations sang in stanza one:

Lo, how a Rose e'er blooming
from tender stem hath sprung!
Of Jesse's lineage coming
as men of old have sung.
It came a floweret bright,
amid the cold of winter,
when half spent was the night.

Twenty years later, those same congregations opened their new hymnals at Christmas and found the following surprise (some wanted to return the gift):

Lo, how a rose *is growing,*
a bloom of finest grace;
the prophets had foretold it:
a branch of Jesse's race
would bear one perfect flow'r
here in the cold of winter
and darkest midnight hour.

Here the move toward a more inclusive expression is much more sophisticated. A bit more subtle than the removal of "men of old," "Jesse's lineage" has become the more inclusive "Jesse's race."

Moving from Christmas carols, we focus on Elizabeth C. Clephane's (1830–1869) gospel hymn "Beneath the Cross of Jesus." The 1978 *Lutheran Book of Worship* editors updated archaic language in the following ways:

Stanza 1: "I fain would take my stand" became "I long to take my stand"

Stanza 2: "Mine eye" became "My eye"
"my smitten heart" became "my contrite heart"
"my own worthlessness" became "my unworthiness" (a
change Southern Baptists had already experienced when
the 1956 *Baptist Hymnal* "replaced" the 1940 *Broadman
Hymnal*)

Stanza 3: "thy shadow" became "your shadow"

We can see now that how these issues were dealt with in the
Lutheran Book of Worship was just the beginning. These issues
would increase in scope and intensity during the remaining years of
the twentieth century. Thomas Kelly's (1769–1854) hymn "Look, ye
saints, the sight is glorious" is presented as evidence that this con-
troversy was still young. That was the title of the hymn in the 1958
Service Book and Hymnal (numbered 114). However, in the 1978
Lutheran Book of Worship, the title had been changed to "Look, the
Sight is Glorious," with the opening line changed to "Look, *oh,* look,
the sight is glorious" (numbered 156). The only other change that
was made was in stanza two where "In the seat of power enthrone
him" had been changed to "*On* the seat of *pow'r* enthrone him."
What remains unchanged is "King of kings and Lord of lords." As
the discussion of the inclusive language issue continued and
deepened, such phrases would be brought into question as being
unnecessarily masculine. Other hymnals, denominational and non-
denominational, would follow the lead of the 1978 *Lutheran Book
of Worship* to one degree or another.

One of the most respected voices in the debate over language
issues was, and remains, that of Brian Wren, the renowned British
hymn writer who now lives in the United States. His focus has been
largely on fresh imagery, challenging an exclusive male imaging of
God, and the promotion of inclusive language in reference to
people. In his book *What Language Shall I Borrow?*[11] Wren expands
on the philosophy and theology that is the basis of his hymnody,
stating early in the book, "I aim to show that every naming of God is
a borrowing from human experience, whether contemporary, traditional, or scriptural, and that though language does not determine
how we think, it shapes and slants thinking and behavior."[12] However, as helpful as his book is, his hymns contain his most effective

---

[11] Brian Wren, *What Language Shall I Borrow? God-Talk in Worship:
A Male Response to Feminist Theology* (New York: Crossroad, 1995).
[12] Ibid., 3.

arguments. Like any art, even the functional poetic art we call hymns, the layers of impact, beginning with what is presented at the surface, serve not only to get the message across at first encounter, but also to implant the message(s) deep in the human soul. The ground-breaking *Lutheran Book of Worship* (1978), contains only one hymn by Brian Wren ("Christ is Alive! Let Christians Sing," numbered 363). But just eleven years later, *The United Methodist Hymnal* (1989), which replaced that denomination's 1964 hymnal, included fourteen of Wren's hymns.

Looking into Wren's stanzas within the newer hymnal we see and hear his strong, representative voice advocating, by example, inclusive language and imaging. Wren's creative work could be considered "agenda-driven" if, indeed, proclaiming the breadth of the gospel, by example, is considered an agenda. This is made clear in his writing, teaching, and conversations, leaving him and others of like mind as open to charges of using the gospel to make a point as are those who oppose "going out of our way" to change and challenge traditional language usage. In Wren's hymn, "God of Many Names" (105), God is presented as "womb and birth of time." In "How Can We Name a Love" (111), it is "a father" who is "kind" and "a mother" who is "strong and sure." "Woman in the Night" (274) is a refreshing gathering and reminder of Jesus' encounters with women from his birth, throughout his ministry, to his death and resurrection. Here, the word "men" appears only once in print, but is sung as often as the refrain is used. This hymn is near, perhaps at, the summit of Wren's hymnography. In "Christ Loves the Church" (590) Wren's expansion of the bounds of imagery is seen in the line "His love outwits us, spinning gold from straw." Here Wren leaves scriptural images long enough to explore truth contained in folk tales. Veterans of the fort, despite the obvious creative poetry, had to look away. Veterans of this front looked deeper.[13]

The work of Wren and many others toward fresh and expanded imagery and inclusive language might well have been received simply as the inevitable evolving of language or the continuing exploration of Scripture and the Christian experience had it

---

[13] For additional reading from the "front" see Gail Ramshaw, *God Beyond Gender: Feminist Christian God-Language* (Minneapolis: Fortress, 1995) and Ruth C. Duck, *Finding Words for Worship: A Guide for Leaders* (Louisville: Westminster John Knox, 1995). The author is not aware of any monographs from the "fort" on this issue, though they certainly may exist.

not been for a particular event in November of 1993. Work toward fresh and inclusive language in worship had been under way for sometime. Indeed, soon after Roman liturgical texts had been translated from Latin into English in response to Vatican II, a "second generation"[14] of translations was undertaken because of the new sensitivity to gender-exclusive language in North America and England. Still, increased activity in the areas of "women's rights" and the "feminist movement," though somewhat similar, had remained separated from the church's inclusive language issues. However, some among the veterans of the fort regarded women's rights, the feminist movement, and inclusive language issues to be one and the same, categorized by the emerging and somewhat inflammatory label, "politically correct."

In November 1993, an ecumenical conference was held in Minneapolis as a celebration of the World Council of Churches' Ecumenical Decade of Churches in Solidarity with Women, which had started in 1988. It was known as the "Re-Imagining" conference. Conference attendees were accused of the heresy of having worshipped the "Goddess" Sophia, Divine Wisdom. Some of the 2000 women who attended the conference referred to it as the second reformation. In response, clergy and laity alike, across denominational lines, protested any official involvement or endorsement their denominations may have exercised related to the conference. This was a significant "artillery" battle in the worship wars with accusations and rebuttals lighting up the sky like tracer rounds in the night. "Heresy," "heresy," "heresy" boomed as a continuing barrage from the fort toward the front. Their tolerance in discussions of the male or female attributes of God ceased when the debate turned to questions about the place, person, and significance of Jesus in Christian theology. Return fire from the front: In the April 6, 1994 issue of *Christian Century,* Catherine Keller of Drew University Theological School in Madison, New Jersey, published an article "Inventing the Goddess: A Study in Ecclesial Backlash." In the article she explained that:

> This Sophia, not a goddess but simply a biblical female metaphor for the Holy, is what a few pastors and theologians have presumed to explore. She has offered a luminous—if rather modest—point of con-

---

[14] For more information concerning the "second generation" of translations after Vatican II, see the article by Christopher J. Walsh, "Minding Our Language: Issues of Liturgical Language Arising in Revision," *Worship* 74:6 (November 2000): 482–503.

nection between traditional biblical language and the feminist evolution of faith.[15]

In the same issue, Joseph D. Small and John P. Burgess, from positions of denominational leadership within the Presbyterian Church (U.S.A.) wrote:

> Clearly, conference rituals attempted to discover and explore new language, not worship a new god. Just as clearly, however, conference rituals used new language in ways that imply worship of a divine manifestation distinctly different from "the one triune God whom alone we worship and serve."

> The language of worship must be shaped with theological and pastoral discernment. Liturgy does far more than ask individuals to consider new possibilities; it engages them in confessional acts and communal practice.[16]

Sophia as a new image and source of new language found little, if any, usage in the worship of mainstream America. Denominational leadership (in any structure and tradition), pastors, and church musicians, in the end, know the power, tolerance levels, and corporate wisdom of the congregation. Battles may rage in other locations and at other "levels," but the deciding battles will be won or lost in the pews.

While another language battle had its day, relatively speaking, it was only a day. The issue of militaristic language reached its most fevered pitch when the committee compiling *The United Methodist Hymnal,* 1989 under Carlton R. Young's experienced and expert leadership, discussed whether or not to include Sabine Baring-Gould's hymn, "Onward, Christian Soldiers." The question was whether or not followers of the Prince of Peace should promote warfare, especially in worship through congregational singing. The debate ranged from issues of peace-making to spiritual warfare described in the Pauline epistles. The debate reached newspapers and pews. The hymn is numbered 575.

---

[15] Catherine Keller, "Inventing the Goddess: A Study in Ecclesial Backlash," *Christian Century* (April 6, 1994): 340–42.

[16] Joseph D. Small and John P. Burgess, "Evaluating 'Re-Imagining': Reformed and Reformulating," *Christian Century* (April 6, 1994): 342f.

Part III

NEGOTIATED PEACE

NINE

Champions of Peace

*It's time to call a truce. Somebody—
most likely the good name of Jesus
our Savior—could get hurt.*

Marv Knox[1]

We want peace, but what are the ramifications of losing a war? This question was asked in the context of the Vietnam War. From the Revolutionary War through World War II, American Christianity assumed that the Prince of Peace was a member of the Reserves, having joined under the name Prince of Victory. It was assumed that, like all American citizens, in time of war, he would don the uniform. Then came Korea and Vietnam and we discovered that the Prince of Peace had not changed his name. We found him waiting for us at the negotiating table.

So, too, in America's worship wars. Veterans of the front and veterans of the fort felt that surely Jesus would help in their campaign toward a victorious establishing of the best, if not one true way of worshiping. But, America's worship wars had no victor. There were losers—witness to the world, reputation, unity—these were but a few of the names chiseled on "the wall."

Both camps, however, had statesmen who knew that no one actually wins a war. They knew that Jesus was always the Prince of Peace waiting at the table, praying still that his followers might be one[2], rebuking the winds of war[3], and saying to all warriors, all veterans, "Be still and know that I am God."[4]

---

[1] "Call a Truce to Music Wars," *Church Musician Today* 4:6 (February 2001): 21.

[2] John 17:11.

[3] Luke 8:22–25.

[4] Ps 46:10.

The Fighter Pilots

Since the Great War (World War I) each war has had its fighter pilots and its submarine captains. Each of these courageous warriors made unique contributions to the war effort. As different as their contributions might appear, the fighter pilots and submarine captains have much in common. They seek peace through victory. Both feel there is something more to be experienced, something unique that can be accomplished beyond the surface. Yet, each has to return. Each is bound, no matter their soaring or diving, to the surface. Though their efforts differ, they share home base. They have equal loyalty and courage.

America's worship wars have also had their "fighter pilots" and "submarine captains," those who soar to the heights of contemporary worship and those who explore the depths of traditional worship. They were seeking peace, not victory. They were exploring and adventuring on our behalf. We shall consider the contributions of selected *representatives* of the "fighter pilots" and "submarine captains" of America's worship wars.

"The measure of the true worshipper that the Father seeks is not the length of his historical tradition or the height of his hands above his head, but the depths of the love in his heart for the Father."[5] These are the words of Graham Kendrick, British songwriter, worship leader, and co-founder of the global March for Jesus, better known as the Jesus Marches. Though British, his England-based ministry has had significant impact in the United States, literally taking his music to the streets and the sanctuaries. His hymns and songs, which number over 300, cross lines drawn by denominational, national, and language differences. His work on the front began when in 1976 he became the Music Director for the British Youth for Christ. The March for Jesus phenomenon began in London in May 1987 with 15,000 participants, grew in the number of events and participants over the years, and continues around the world, even to the time of this writing. He is firmly established as a supplier of creative methods and "portable," contemporary songs of worship and social justice for veterans of the front. Yet, he is an ally of the veterans of the fort, writing songs that look and sing like hymns, that deal with traditional subjects of worship and

---

[5] Graham Kendrick, *The Collection* (Great Britain: Kingsway Music Limited, 1992), Foreword.

renewal. Many of his songs, such as his popular "Shine, Jesus, Shine," serve both groups, becoming common ground and offering a bit of rest and relaxation from the worship wars.

Through his songs, the warring parties are reminded of how fresh the breeze is when we sing together, how pleasant the memories are of singing as once in the past, and offering believable hope that such unity can be regained. We know the songs function inside and outside the fort and thus the singers feel a part of both enterprises.

The style of Kendrick's congregational songs, something between a praise chorus and a hymn, opened the way for the ballads of Gen-X worship. His extension of the portable praise chorus into a vehicle for telling the story honors the front-line work of those who first moved into Praise and Worship. Yet, it is that very telling of the story that causes traditional worshipers to see his songs as extensions or the further development of hymns. It is not a happy accident when Christian worshippers "find" each other. The work of the Holy Spirit matches and supports the prayers of Jesus, including his prayer that his disciples might come together as one. Congregational singing has always been, and is by its very nature, an agent for unification. It is misuse and manipulation that cause congregational song to be divisive. The musical and non-musical gather to sing praise and prayer. Hymns from a wide variety of Christian traditions are bound together in denominational-specific hymnals and non-denominational hymnals. Hymns and other congregational song become the shared property of multiple generations. Christians from a wide variety of nations unite in shared congregational song. We are, indeed, marching to Zion and we can march together. The songs do, indeed, abound. Graham Kendrick, through word and deed, work and influence, is writing and encouraging the songs of street and sanctuary that invite unity and offer peace.

Another of America's worship wars' "fighter pilots" is Sally Morgenthaler (they let women fly now). Like a good fighter pilot she dropped out of the sun, unseen, right into the middle of the battle. Her book *Worship Evangelism*[6] combines in its title the very banners of the two camps of veterans. Coming from the camp whose tents are pitched on the front, she connects with those from the fort who can get past her book's title, by stating that worship is to be worship. Worship is about God, of God, and for God.

[6] Sally Morgenthaler, *Worship Evangelism: Inviting Unbelievers into the Presence of God* (Grand Rapids, Mich.: Zondervan, 1995).

Worship is the work of believers, but—worship is intriguing, perhaps can even be magnetic, to those who do not yet claim Jesus as Lord. Because of her weaving together the desire of the veterans of the front for worship to be evangelistic and the desire of the veterans of the fort for worship to have no other agenda than worship, we can forgive her title's reinforcement of the idea that worship takes us into the presence of God. Indeed, the veil has been torn in two and God is always with us. When we come to worship we acknowledge God's presence in a reverent and focused way, but we do not come from "outside" where we live to "inside" where God lives. Indeed Sally Morgenthaler and I have had this conversation in person and found ourselves in agreement. That is common ground. The occurrence is not uncommon, nor should it be surprising. "Come now, let us reason together says the Lord" (Isaiah 1:18 NIV) isn't a difficult verse to memorize. True, the phrase is translated "argue it out" in the NRSV, but even that translation presents an honest step forward toward peace. That is significant conversation and community. Our conversation, based on the common ground presented in contemporary worship terminology, was a small glimmer of the glorious light that can shine in Christian worship if all the veterans, we brothers and sisters, will cease fire and move to the negotiating table. Did the word *table,* just read, call forth images of Christians gathered around the communion table, gathered around in our various forms of sacred symbol? Sally Morgenthaler calls us to the peace table by reminding us that the real thing is magnetic. Real believers (with all the sinful duality of knowing right and doing wrong) worshiping the real God (in three persons) are different from anything else not-yet believers encounter in "the world." We should know that and keep worship focused on God for the sake of the world. Sally Morgenthaler helps us see that, and what we see looks like home for veterans of the fort and veterans of the front. We discover that we veterans all have the same home address. We are family and community, but now and then, we might sing our songs of heaven in the language of earth, dropping a little grain in the field for others to pick up as we go home to eat our bread.

The Submarine Captains

One of the first of these warriors and explorers of the deep was Donald Hustad. He dared to admit, in print, that he was a "schizophrenic musician."[7] In practice that was an understatement. He served as organist for the Billy Graham Crusades (the front) and as Professor of Church Music at The Southern Baptist Theological Seminary in Louisville, Kentucky (the fort), at the time the nearest thing Southern Baptists had to a music conservatory.[8] Yet, as a person, despite the confession, Don Hustad was, and is, a Christ-follower of one heart and mind. His statement allowed the rest of us who were trying to be effective church musicians at a much lower level of recognition, to exhale the great sigh of relief, "Yes, me too."

His is a philosophy and theology of church music that anticipated "the sproutings of widespread, fairly radical changes in worship patterns and music styles"[9] and gave us a way of thinking and an understanding of worship and church music ministry that would give us a core to return to when the going got rough out on the edges. It was our work as ministers to remember and to revisit the core. His second book, noted in the previous sentence, helped us find our way back to our center. It was there at the center that we could meet for negotiations with our brothers and sisters from the other camp and then venture back to our forts with at least a fragile peace.

As long as we admitted our *music* schizophrenia we could negotiate our *worship* schizophrenia. It was when we were forced to choose sides to get and/or keep a particular place of ministry (or out of actual personal conviction) that we denied our schizophrenia and went to war. Like families living in a Civil War border state, brothers left for both camps. The writings of Don Hustad called to us, reminding us of that peaceful place where, though we didn't always agree, we got along by agreeing to disagree; that place where we could admit our schizophrenia and other maladies, and find acceptance and understanding. The voice and writings of Don Hustad are still with us, but war is another world, and we have learned to ignore the tug toward home.

Harold M. Best, former dean of the conservatory of music at Wheaton College in Illinois, wrote *Music Through the Eyes of*

---

[7] Donald P. Hustad, *Jubilate! Church Music in the Evangelical Tradition* (Carol Stream, Ill.: Hope Publishing Company, 1981), vii.

[8] This analysis rises as a compliment from the deepest respect and admiration.

[9] Donald P. Hustad, *Jubilate II. Church Music in Worship and Renewal* (Carol Stream, Ill.: Hope Publishing Company, 1993), xiii.

Faith[10] and for a moment stopped the war. It is not his fault that it
started up again. Much of America's worship wars have been
fought with the pride of having found the most excellent way of
worshipping. Veterans of the fort were protecting it and veterans
of the front were discovering it. Some congregations and/or their
ministers declared their excellence or declared their intentions to
obtain that excellence by being like some other congregation
deemed to have achieved excellence according to a chosen stan-
dard. Harold Best reminds us that "excellence is not being better
than somebody else, nor is it even being like him, her, or them. . . .
We cannot become better than we once were with other people's
gifts."[11] Two pages later he reminds us "excellence is authenticity."

Like God commanding Moses to throw down his staff, Best
calls on us to throw down all the personal strength and identity
that music has come to symbolize in our individual lives and worship and in our community life and worship. He admonishes us,
instead, to act on faith. And, like Moses, we see what we have
been leaning on for the snake that it is, slithery and, perhaps, poi-
sonous. Then, reading Best's words and hearing God's voice, we
pick it up again. We reclaim the music and it becomes the rod of
God. Shall we who limp into worship leaning on God's staff, swing
those sacred sticks at each other when we leave the sanctuary—or
gym? Harold Best has shown us the negotiating table and stands
ready to place a chair under us as we sit. Some do sit. Music
through the eyes of faith and the worship it enhances also seen
through the eyes of faith will see God first. No longer blinded by
musical pride and prejudice (with apologies), we will open our
eyes to the tragedy of worship wars and bind up wounds that we
may have inflicted. We (veterans of both camps) must adjust to
the light. In his "Introduction," Best reminds us music making is
subordinate to and informed by the larger doctrines of creation,
worship, offering, faith, grace, stewardship, redemptive witness,
excelling, and love (p. 7). Veterans of war should know about
being subordinate and about being informed or molded by larger
doctrines. Best helps us see that a negotiated peace in the worship
wars will only come about as we see music, our call to music ministry, our worship, and each other through the eyes of faith. In an
address to the American Choral Directors Association National

---

[10] Harold M. Best, *Music Through the Eyes of Faith* (San Francisco:
Harper, 1993).
[11] Ibid., 111.

Convention in Chicago in 1999, Harold Best included this contribution to negotiated peace for America's worship wars:

> Once we get our structures and artifacts out of the way only to regain them in the Light; once we take the burden off the gifts and lay it on to the Giver; once we fully realize that the gift is not responsible for our worship, but the Giver is; once we understand that God alone is both Means and End, Author and Finisher, Alpha and Omega; once these things become gradually clearer; and once we see and remain in the Light, we will find it shining on common ground, the common ground of godly and authentic worship, a continuum of action upon action, faithfully and knowingly made into offering after offering, straight through this life and on into eternity.[12]

Marva J. Dawn and Sally Morgenthaler are considered by many to be on opposing sides in the worship wars. A better analysis is that they, while starting at different points on the continuum of worship style, are working toward the same end, the same goal. Both want worship to "truly praise God and form us and the community to reach out to the world"![13] In her books, especially *Reaching Out Without Dumbing Down*,[14] and in her conference leading and preaching, Marva Dawn adds her voice to the declaration that worship is for the one and only God. Neither its focus nor its purpose is to be shared or diluted. She has alerted worship leaders to how easily that can happen. Her message helps establish the agenda that needs to be addressed if a negotiated peace is to be achieved. Whether or not the negotiators agree with her assessments, the issues she raises get at the heart of the matter. Anything other than the points she raises remain too close to the surface, hiding or avoiding the issues that cause war or allow peace. Is worship being "used"? Is it being diluted or dumbed down because of subtle, perhaps even subconscious, influences that are more related to the kingdom of this world that the kingdom of heaven? Has worship been sidetracked or kidnapped (not her words) in order to accomplish something instead of or in addition to worship? Talk about *these* things, she insists. Do not hide

---

[12]Harold M. Best. "Authentic Worship & Faithful Music Making," available at www.ACDAonline.org/ncmw/authenticworship.html.

[13]Personal inscription by Marva J. Dawn in the author's personal copy of *Reaching Out without Dumbing Down*.

[14]Marva J. Dawn, *Reaching Out without Dumbing Down: A Theology of Worship for the Turn-of-the-Century Culture* (Grand Rapids, Mich.: Eerdmans, 1995).

them. Do not protect them from the light of day and debate. These issues are the basis of any potential peace because they are the basis of the war. If her suggestions make the reader/worship leaders angry, those persons should ask why they are angry. Does worship *trans*form or *con*form? Is the back of worship being broken because of misplaced or overloaded burdens? A negotiated peace can be and must be attained, but these questions lie across the path. The negotiators, that is to say, the worship leaders of note and influence from the front and the fort must rise to the answers that wait. Marva J. Dawn risks ridicule and misunderstanding for the cause of peace and an end to America's worship wars. She challenges strategies of worship and calls veterans of the fort and veterans of the front to a theology of worship; to a community of veterans, indeed, no longer warriors. She invites us to exchange the noise of war for silence. "It is impossible for our inner selves to be prepared to be open to God and receptive to God's Word until we *silence* [author's italics] our sinful selves—our efforts to be in control, to manipulate everything and everyone to accomplish our own purposes."[15]

Robert E. Webber is another of the worship wars' "submarine captains." In his many books, speeches, and conference sessions, he has given us the very useful image of convergence, "the phenomenon of convergence in modern liturgical and charismatic churches."[16] He knows, by experience, both liturgical worship and "free worship." In giving us the phrase, the concept, and the experience of *convergence* of worship styles, elements, and theologies, he blesses and helps facilitate efforts toward peace. More than that, he has presented the prelude, the introit, for the worship we will experience "on the margin" (see the Epilogue of this book). By showing us that worship is a verb,[17] not a noun, he encourages us to stop thinking of worship as something we watch or mold or use. He challenges us to understanding worship as something we "do." The next step on this path after "doing" is "being." It is the path toward peace. When we are "being" our worship, when we

---

[15] Ibid., 266.

[16] Robert E. Webber, *Signs of Wonder: The Phenomenon of Convergence in Modern Liturgical and Charismatic Churches* (Nashville: Abbott Martyn, 1992).

[17] Webber's contributions to our understanding of this concept are presented most effectively in Robert E. Webber, *Worship Is a Verb: Eight Principles for Transforming Worship.* (Peabody, Mass.: Hendrickson, 1992).

are living our lives as acts of worship, Christians will no longer be at war with each other. It is rather obscene to imagine sinners, saved by the grace of God, squabbling at the foot of the cross, slapping at each other before the throne, arguing over who will sit at the right hand, in the presence of the Redeemer.

Webber further encourages peace by championing "the biblical sequence of Preparation, Word, Table, and Dismissal as a pattern for spiritual renewal [as a] structure [that] provides a context in which the struggle between order [liturgical worship] and freedom [worship in the 'free church'] can take place authentically."[18] A common foundation, based on Scripture, with customized "super-structure" based on doctrine is a formula for worshiping the Prince of Peace, in peace. It cultivates a community of unity and diversity, two beautiful aspects of Christianity.

War is fought by the soldiers. Peace is negotiated by the leaders, by the politicians. If it were up to the "grunts" on the front line, peace would happen immediately. Doing what they are trained and led to do, the warriors keep fighting. Leaders must see the folly, want the peace, confess the futility, negotiate the peace, and declare that the war is over. These "fighter pilots" and "submarine captains," and those they represent, are writing the leadership manuals for peace. Will the leaders read them?

---

[18] Ibid., p. 13.

TEN

How Do We Train Worship Leaders?

*How can we educate today so that
"the day after" will be a time of
compassion rather than combat?*

Parker J. Palmer[1]

As Educators Who Minister

At the time of the convening of the Second Vatican Council, much of the church music education in the seminaries, colleges, and universities of the United States was toward the end of preparing young ministers to educate the congregation. The music of worship was seen as an offering or a sacrifice to God. Church musicians were to equip and lead their congregations to make costly offerings to God, nothing cheap. If individual members of the congregation were not musically talented, they were to be encouraged toward the "widow's mite," making the best joyful noise possible. Working to produce a worthy musical sacrifice was the responsibility of instrumentalists, choir members, soloists, and the congregation. Church musicians were trained to oversee such endeavors. They were to exhibit the heart of a minister, but with the exactness and goals of a highly trained musician. Interestingly, given the widely differing potential of individual congregations, these well-trained musicians were often successful. Often the more highly educated led clinics and workshops to pass their training and understanding along to the less musically educated but none the less talented or committed who had music (worship was still

---

[1] *To Know As We Are Known: Education as a Spiritual Journey* (San Francisco: Harper, 1983), 9–10.

assumed, not delineated) leadership responsibilities in their, often, smaller parishes.

One of the overarching assumptions in this atmosphere of training educators who would minister at the parish level was that if you can do Bach, you can do Peterson. But, if you can only do Peterson, you are stuck at that level of church music. This proverb was meant to warm the ministerial hearts of the ministers of music in training. Ministers would move toward Peterson to join their congregations and then, eventually, move the congregation closer to Bach. J. S. Bach hasn't needed introducing since the days of Mendelssohn. But the proverb speaks only if one knows the identity of John W. Peterson (b. 1921). The students knew. Having written widely received vocal solos in the 1940s and 1950s, he was the composer of Christmas and Easter cantatas that took blue-collar and many white-collar evangelical congregations by storm in the 1960s and into the mid-1970s. For some volunteer choirs his cantatas were a bit of stretch, but even for them, the Peterson style of composition became familiar and the experience of learning and presenting the cantata was worth the effort of rehearsal. Part of the joy of each new season was the anticipation of the new "Peterson cantata." For the Ministers of Music, however, the acceptable performance of a "Peterson cantata" was a building block toward a Bach cantata, no matter the number of additional stops there might be along the way.

I remember as a young college student beginning my studies in church music in the summer of 1969, entering the classroom where a beloved professor taught music theory. Someone had written a hypothetical test question on the blackboard. The professor saw the chalk graffiti and smiled, but didn't erase it. It was an indication that the student who had written the joke was "getting it," even though the professor was very much a committed churchman. The student's tongue-in-cheek quiz: "Explain why Peterson's cantatas are superior to those of Bach." A few years later at a church music conference held on the campus of Sacramento State University, one of my fellow conferees asked our conference leader, Dr. John W. Peterson, if he had ever heard of the term "Peterson cantata"? His answer was something to the effect, "You mean one of those mediocre, formula, pedestrian, seasonal collections? Yes, I'm familiar with the term, but I would like to tell you something." Then this composer who had studied at Moody Bible Institute *and* the American Conservatory of Music in Chicago said, (this is closer to a direct quote) "I don't want people who work all week to have to work at worshipping on Sunday." His statement flew in the face of what I had learned about working to give our very best efforts in the use of music in worship. I sensed a crack in the ground beneath church music; a crack that would someday become a chasm. What I had actually encountered was my first creative tension dichotomy; a question I was only going to be able to "live," not answer. I smiled at myself and the irony of it all when I read the following quote a few years later in John W. Peterson's autobiography, *The Miracle Goes On.* Speaking of God leading him to go to the conservatory instead of seminary after his studies at Moody, Peterson wrote:

> The reason became clear only years later. Without that concentrated education in the classics, and without the guidance of brilliant teachers and composers at the conservatory, I would have been ill equipped to tackle the larger choral works which lay far in my future.[2]

He, too, was studying Bach in order to do "Peterson cantatas." The line drawn between high church and low church, Bach and Peterson (later Bach and Bill Gaither), was not as distinct as I had been led to believe by my education. But the people in the pews of the congregations I served early in my ministry, and many more like them, had no trouble seeing the line and were quick to point it out to me if I happened to step over it. Peterson was their man and their music. Little did we know then that dealing with differences related to high and low church worship would prove to be important training for the time when a congregation's worship style options would grow from a couple to a half-dozen or more.

While this divergence between the education of the Minister of Music and the realities of the "average" local evangelical congregation resulted in a few skirmishes, it did not grow into a full-blown war. Young Ministers of Music mellowed, and congregational leaders were somewhat patient, knowing that "it would take a couple of years" for their well-educated musician to "get over" *his* college and seminary training. Yes, seminary. Southern Baptists have six seminaries that include masters degrees, some doctorates as well, in church music. The education of church musicians had been a high priority with Southern Baptists for many years. If there was a need to "get over" seminary training it was because of the

---

[2]John W. Peterson, *The Miracle Goes On: An Autobiography* (Grand Rapids, Mich.: Zondervan, 1976), 151.

immaturity of the young ministers of music, not the supposed indifference of the faculty.

Seminary training in church music built upon and under-girded the traditional and "formal" training the young minister of music had experienced in college. In fact, it was not uncommon for remedial courses to be required of those whose seminary entrance exams indicated that the student had not learned all he or she should have about the fundamentals of music theory and history while in college—a practice not fully appreciated by the college professors or the students who had to take what they referred to as "dumb-dumb" courses.

While it is true that the music education or appreciation skirmishes between new church music graduates and their first churches did not escalate into battle, the bridge across the gap was often less than sturdy. This was especially true when congregations warmed up to new ideas in contemporary church music much sooner than their learned leaders. While they did not want the music of the street and rock concert in their worship, neither did they want the academy's "high-brow" stuff.

What wonderful people, the congregation. Frustrating and plodding as they may be, the wisdom and the mind of Christ in the midst of the body of Christ cannot be ignored. This is why the veteran of the front eventually returns to the fort and why the wisest of the young graduates of the academy often loosen up a bit in the fort.

As Tradespeople

Some did not take lightly the good-natured joke about it taking a minister of music two years to "get over" seminary training. While the ministers of music in the mega-churches were gaining celebrity status and the church growth movement was creating local church icons, a number of would-be ministers of music were questioning the traditional educational route to the music ministry. It was soon observed that people graduating from college had a better chance of being called to a large church if, instead of going to seminary, they would sign-on to a two- or three-year internship under the tutelage of one of the mega-church "heroes" (not a self-designated term). The math seemed simple: spend three years earning a Master's degree in church music and then begin your "climb up" from a small "starter" church or spend perhaps only two years as an intern in a mega-church and move laterally to another big church. The intern "graduate" could begin at a larger church than the seminary graduate might ever serve. While the relatively few intern slots could not overtake the seminaries, their shortcut to the highest peaks could not be ignored. What did they learn in the mega-church that they were not being taught in the seminary? What did the seminary offer that could be held up as worth the sacrifice of time, money, and potential? The answers seemed to lie somewhere between the perceived mega-churches' shortsighted vision of the successful Sunday and the academy's perceived backward stare for the purpose of building a music foundation for the future. Of course, each side's perception of the other was somewhat distorted.

The mega-churches did not look back and were not concerned. The seminaries felt compelled to adjust. Not to reclaim the few who had opportunities to choose the intern option, but to regain the confidence of the veterans of the fort and the potential students they could influence. Contemporary ensembles were formed in many colleges and seminaries to stand beside traditional performing groups. Popular contemporary musicals were injected into the performance repertory of "oratorio" choirs, mingling Gaither with Handel, Haydn, and Brahms. Electronic keyboard labs took their place alongside organs and pianos. Seminary administrators (often former pastors) and students studying for the pastorate thought the changes good, as far as they went. In many cases, however, church music professors and "serious" church music students saw only dangerous, if necessary, concessions, buying the right to continue on the proper course (pun acknowledged). There were well-intentioned efforts to bring the "ministerial" and music students together in practical administration and worship courses, but the divide was too deep. Further, everyone knew that, in most cases, the administrators and "preacher boys" had the musically uneducated congregations on their side. The worship wars were embryonic differences of opinion at this point, accepted separations of academic focuses.

The embryos were being incubated in the multi-layered discussions and concerns about whether seminaries should be more like universities or vocational schools. It seemed that, like a local congregation, a seminary's intent or position on the issue could most easily and readily be declared by its music. The presidents of the seminaries were former pastors, not former ministers of music. The Church Music School, Division, or Department's part in creating the image could be quickly, effectively, and fairly easily (though not always painlessly) accomplished. Pastors and Ministers of Music, even those in training, serve the same congregation, understand the congregation's needs and potential, and, in the best cases, share the same vision. Differences arise in visions of *how* music should be employed in the life and work of that congregation. Those same differences followed pastors and ministers of music into their new careers as educators at the college and seminary levels.

Schools Responding to Congregations

Somehow, the fact that the college and seminary system of church music education just described was the very system that produced the composers and worship leaders of the contemporary worship movement seemed to go unnoticed. Instead, that system was frequently criticized as slowing down, even opposing, the development of contemporary worship and its music. Extreme pressure was placed upon the music schools in Baptist colleges and seminaries to catch up to the times, to educate toward contemporary worship. This pressure was not limited to Baptist schools. They are singled out here because of the author's personal experience. The pressure was coming from pastors of local churches through their former colleagues who were now in positions of leadership in the schools and through denominational hierarchy. Pastors rushing to participate in the church growth movement via contemporary worship wanted the indirect validation of the education system and wanted "Worship Leaders" (no longer "Ministers of Music") who didn't have to work through or "get over" the church music education that had been traditionally offered at their schools. To be fair, it should be noted that many ministers of music joined the contemporary worship movement of their own accord. Not all were coerced in order to keep their jobs. The old argument that to do Peterson, Gaither, or contemporary well, the church musician needed to be able to do Bach well, was now ridiculed as resistant, old paradigm, and inefficient. Fad, trend, relevance, selling the inheritance of the future for the stew of next Sunday; accusations flew back and forth between sanctuary and classroom, studio and administrative suite. Students aligned with one side or the other out of conviction or convenience. Acknowledging the contemporary in traditional courses and ensembles rather than making major changes in the curriculum was often seen as being passive aggressive. Where professors worshiped, not by denomination, but congregation, became issues when the question was asked, "How can they teach contemporary church music and worship if their membership, thus heart, is in a traditional setting?" The skirmishes became battles—battles complete with casualties.

Debates about high church vs. low church and practical vs. academic certainly were not new to America's worship wars, indeed, they significantly predate Vatican II. But in the context of the worship wars, they can be seen as adding to the intensity, breadth, and depth of the wars. Any educational approach or methodology was seen as endorsing and cultivating one side or the other (contemporary or traditional, the front or the fort). Neutrality was not allowed or recognized. Neither was the debate allowed to remain within the confines of worship. To speak of worship is to speak of an important aspect of theology and that is always true, but to speak of worship was to assign worship and evangelism places on a priority list. To speak of worship was to comment on the well-known worship style of a particularly influential church or pastor. To speak of worship was to comment on whether or not popular trends were valid.

Higher Education Responds

In denominational settings, especially, institutions of higher learning have a certain responsibility and accountability to their constituencies. Few would argue with that. Many, however, would argue at the point of whether or not that means that the school should follow the church in immediate lock-step in every instance of experiment, change, or innovation. Schools and churches approach those endeavors, sometimes in similar fashion, sometimes at different levels. The slow pace of curricula changes, whether or not it is by design, serves an important purpose. The pace is a built-in safeguard against hasty changes. What a student learns in college, university, and seminary is foundational more than it is utilitarian. In a congregation the learning is more utilitarian than foundational. Higher education is to help the young minister through a lifetime. Yet, there must be some weekly evidence of immediately useful application.

What is learned in the setting of the congregation is to help the minister through a week, month, quarter, or year. Both time frames and levels are crucial. Vernon Davis, Dean of the Logsdon School of Theology, Hardin-Simmons University, Abilene, Texas wrote:

> If the scholarship of discovery and integration avoids application, it will be shunned in a world obsessed by the demand for immediate relevance. . . . On the other hand, the scholarship of application alone leads to theological education by workshop and the continuing search for that elusive method that can guarantee results in doing church successfully.[3]

Workshop, Symposium, and Conference

The quote from Dr. Davis introduces an educational format (workshop) that, as in other instances, predates the worship wars, yet played an important role in the worship wars. Publishing companies, individual authors and composers, music distributors and other entities stepped in between the application-focused veterans of the front and the foundation-focused veterans of the fort and provided a forum for discussion of current issues, products, and methodologies. These one- to three-day events were focused and immediately relevant. The conferee went home with a plastic or canvass bag of materials and ideas that could be applied immediately. Obviously, such an event is most helpful as a life-long learning event, a freshening of ideas, and a source of encouragement. But three dangers lurked. One: the idea that something that could be so helpful in just three days could surely be immensely more helpful if it continued for three years. Two: some of the conference leaders sent the attendees home with ideas that could only have disastrous results if applied immediately (such as the abandonment of hymns, hymnals, choirs, etc.). Three: the idea that something that works *somewhere* can work *anywhere*. These dangers were not always, perhaps not even often, the fault of the conference leaders. Indeed, conference leaders such as Rick Warren, pastor of the Saddleback Community Church in Orange County, California, often warned their audience to make proper variations in application.

---

[3] Vernon Davis, "The Unsettled Landscape of Theological Education," *Review & Expositor: A Consortium Baptist Theological Journal* 95:4 (Fall 1998): 486–87.

Throughout the closing decades of the twentieth century, church-related institutions of higher learning adopted the workshop or symposium format to address current issues without disrupting the necessary foundational elements of their curricula. These proved to be occasions of "R and R" (rest and relaxation) from the worship wars for the schools. They could show that they were aware of current issues and trends. They could have the spokespersons for contemporary worship on campus, yet in settings that were perhaps friendlier and more familiar than the formal classroom. Many veterans of the front and the fort saw these events as positive. However, some veterans of the front saw them as smoke screens, designed not to hide movement, but to hide the absence of movement—accusations, rebuttal, battles, war.

Drastic Response or Creative Response?

A few schools that were subject to severe scrutiny and a few schools that saw the worship wars as opportunities to move to the cutting edge of education ventured into new and controversial territory. Some ventured farther than others. The advent of Doctor of Ministry degree programs allowed "worship studies" to be presented as an area of concentration. In its infancy, the Doctor of Ministry degree was attacked as weak, unnecessary, and second rate—these accusations, of course, in comparison with the Th.D. or Ph.D. As the twentieth century neared its end, the "D.Min." became fully respected. Be that as it may, it gave credence to worship as a separate or particular focus of study. Other new degrees began to emerge, not just with a worship concentration option, but with "worship" actually in the degree title: Master of Arts in Worship Leadership, Master of Theological Studies in Worship, and Doctor of Worship Studies are examples. These degrees exist in reputable environments (seminaries and at least one independent institute). But questions flocked to each new unveiling, questions of credibility in actual church and/or academic settings. Courses, bibliographies, and teachers were/are quite respectable, many of the first order, but something was troubling, not to the point of causing battles to flare, but something a bit unsettling to the peace. What about accreditation by traditional accrediting agencies? What about the "worship" of worship wars having its own set of degrees, apart from traditional music and theology degrees? Did this mean that the "war" of worship wars was also being promoted? Did this mean that the traditional degree paths and areas of study were now passé? Were all of the new degrees solid? If not, would the churches know the difference? Master of Divinity degrees with Church Music emphases and Master of Religious Education degrees with Church Music emphases had also appeared, but they were within accepted, traditional boundaries.[4] These innovations often challenged those boundaries. Challenging boundaries, like oxygen, are necessary for life, but also an essential component for combustion.

Academia's unsettled peace was, in actual practice, sophisticated war. The pressure to be relevant led to inevitable comparisons. Potential students, students, alumni, and employers (churches and schools) want to be assured that the education received is strong, valid, and effective. It is common knowledge that in a pressured environment, comparisons are not always a search for constructive criticism. They are often a search for validation. Institutions, be they a school or a particular program of study within that school, will fight for their lives, if they sense that they are being threatened. Proponents of new ideas and methodologies will fight for their right to exist. Existence and recognition issues that affect communities, traditions, and futures have started or contributed to more than one war. Parker Palmer sounded the warning:

> So teachers who try to create a space in which obedience to truth is practiced must do battle with a host of external enemies. . . . Institutions are projections of what goes on in the human heart. To ignore the inward sources of our educational dilemmas is only to objectify the problem—and thereby multiply it.[5]

Church-related academia has a moral obligation, indeed, a *spiritual* obligation to lead in the search for a negotiated end to the worship wars and then, a productive peace.

---

[4]For a short but interesting comment in this area from a respected church music educator and practitioner, see Carlton R. Young, "An Alternative Model For the Education of the Church Musician," in *Duty and Delight: Routley Remembered, A Memorial Tribute to Erik Routley (1917–1982)* (ed. Carlton R. Young; Carol Stream, Ill.: Hope Publishing Company, 1985), 97–100.

[5]Palmer, *To Know As We Are Known,* 10.

ELEVEN

Cold War or New Order?

> *It follows that neither a denomination*
> *separately nor all the denominations linked*
> *together in some kind of federal unity*
> *or "reconciled diversity" can be the agents*
> *of a missionary confrontation with*
> *our culture, for the simple reason that*
> *they are themselves the outward and*
> *visible signs of an inward and spiritual*
> *surrender to the ideology of our culture.*
>
> Lesslie Newbigin[1]

Those are fightin' words—the words in italics above, even if a missionary wrote them. "Surrender" is not a word that was/is often used in the worship wars. If doctrine matters, then denominations matter. Newbigin's statement is related to a much simpler one by Gary Burge, "My students and friends are migrating to new spiritual homes."[2] How can this happen when the doctrines upon which denominations are built include such eternally important subjects as salvation? War, for all its maps and strategies in rear echelon "war rooms," is often quite confusing and always much more messy in the field. In the worship wars, tradition, theology, doctrine, innovation, evangelism, social justice, preferences, identities, all of these may be perceived as being "under attack" at any one time. In that environment, to speak of one issue can be misinterpreted as devaluing the others. That adds to the fury. Yet, worship seems to rise above its worship war fury. Worship cannot

---

[1] *Foolishness to the Greeks: The Gospel and Western Culture* (Grand Rapids, Mich.: Eerdmans, 1986), 145–46.

[2] Gary M. Burge, "Missing God at Church? Why So Many Are Rediscovering Worship in Other Traditions," *Christianity Today* (October 6, 1997): 27.

be divorced from theology. That's why worship wars are so intense. Ironically, it is also the hope for significant "re-ordering" of intra-Christian alliances and alignments. The cold war among Christians, made hot by the worship wars, can be resolved into a united front for the kingdom of heaven as we confront the issues related to our mission to the kingdom of this world. Denominational doctrines will always matter, perhaps not in the future in the same ways as in the past. More and more, our doctrinal beliefs will be acknowledged as the place from which we come to meet other Christians for the purpose of solving problems within and confronting issues without. Our denominational doctrines will be the contributions we make to such solutions and unity, not our reason to turn away. Perhaps our denominational, doctrinal, differences will become gifts we give to each other instead of possessions we protect or conceal from each other.

If America's worship wars are to move from cold war (we smile as we strategize) to a new order (Christian-against-Christian strategizing ceases), America's worshiping Christians are going to have to ask questions equally deep and profound. To an extent, some of the questions are already being asked, but often simply from shell-shocked battle fatigue. We want the worship wars to end. That is not enough. We must approach the immediate difficult questions and then their underlying questions from a desire to create the most Christ-like new world order in worship that is possible. For example, in light of religious pluralism and rampant materialism ("What can *you* do for your country in this new war? Go shopping!"), I would ask my fellow Baptists, "Are liturgical Christian traditions the 'enemy' or 'allies'? Are Pentecostal Christians the enemy?" "Liturgical" and "Pentecostal" are worship war silhouettes, similar in function to silhouettes that help one identify enemy aircraft from a distance. And what of those outside Christianity? Are they to be "targeted" by Christian zeal or engaged and embraced by Christ-like love? Christian worship has its roots in Jewish worship. Shall Christianity sever itself from its roots or let its lifeblood circulate throughout its whole body, even its roots? Christian ministry and evangelism have their roots in Christian worship. Shall our ministry and evangelism replace its life-source, worship, or shall worship be allowed to nourish those endeavors? How we worship as Christians affects everything else we do as Christians.

Since Vatican II, Christian worship in the United States has been caught up in America's transition from modernity to post-modernity. In a sense, James Hunter's cultural war "traditionalists" and "progressives" are our worship wars' "veterans of the fort" and "veterans of the front."[3] In 1997 Robert Nash Jr. wrote:

> Both groups of Christians face quite a dilemma. Christianity is an exclusive faith that, for hundreds of years, has claimed to possess the only true path to God. It is unique among the major world religions in its insistence that human beings must accept its truth-claims in order to attain salvation. This exclusivity has been increasingly questioned in recent years as religious diversity has increased. Traditionalist and progressivist Christians have responded quite differently to this *threat* [Author's italics].[4]

Threat? Yes, at a deep, core level. But with the core intact, there is much room for learning, sharing, and cooperative effort. If all we do is take a desperate, defensive stance with our backs against that core, we fail to venture out into issues of justice, working with other Christians, believers in the God of Abraham, and generally, peaceful, generous people to do the ministry to which God has called us. Young adult Christians seem to understand that kind of thinking and have felt a freedom to engage in a sort of denominational migration or "church shopping," a wandering around inside safe confines for worship and ministry opportunities that support it.

Post-Denominationalism or Re-Denominationalism?

I think God is trying to tell us something. Through the church-shopping and denominational migration of young adult Christians and through bitter in-house denominational theo-political wars, we are being forced to re-think denominationalism. It should not surprise us that worship is *a*, if not, *the* focal point. In my own tradition, Southern Baptists have been at war for several decades. We have seen people leave by choice and force Baptist congregations, Baptist service agencies, and the faculties of Baptist seminaries. We have seen "Ma S.B.C." birth "baby 'Bs,'" much like "Ma Bell" birthed "baby Bells." These "baby 'Bs,'" both the left and the right of the litter, bear a family resemblance to their mother, but try from

---

[3] James Davison Hunter, *Culture Wars: The Struggle to Define America* (New York: Basic Books, 1991), 44–45.

[4] Robert N. Nash Jr., *An 8-Track Church in a CD World: The Modern Church in the Postmodern World* (Macon, Ga.: Smyth & Helwys, 1997), 22.

birth to assert their independence. And, indeed, they do, but not to the point of rejecting their family name. In fact, all claim to be the re-birth of the original. One can hope and pray that these birth pains are moving toward a day, when Baptists (no longer using "given names"), overwhelmed by a renewed awareness of the world's need, turn old swords into new plows. As with Baptists, while we're hoping and praying, why not with all Christians as well; individuals, yet keeping the family name, uniting in ministry for the good of *The* Kingdom's work? I cannot escape Jesus' prayer in John 17. Jesus, the Word, who was there from the/our beginning, who knows our individual giftedness and sinfulness, still prayed, "make them one" (vv. 6–11). Jesus, too, must surely pray without ceasing.

Re-denominationalism does not wish to loose doctrinal nor worship distinctions. At its best it will see them as the beauty of diversity and the gifts of unity.

Denominational Migration and Church Shopping

There have always been those who have moved from one congregation to another within the same town. It was the common (certainly not always correct) understanding that they were either angry or didn't want to work. But the numbers of migratory members have grown to the point that the situation demands analysis.

> Relying on a unique poll of nearly 300,000 worshipers sitting in pews on or about April 29 last year [2001], a nation-wide survey found that nearly a quarter of them had switched congregations in the past five years.[5]

The newcomers are returnees and first-timers. A number of studies and books have focused on this phenomenon. Two of the more interesting and widely received of these are William D. Hendricks' *Exit Interviews*[6] and Robert E. Webber's *Evangelicals on the Canterbury Trail.*[7] The reasons for leaving the church or

---

[5]John Dart, "Church Shoppers—Many Newcomers in the Pews," *Christian Century* (January 30–February 6, 2002): 13

[6]William D. Hendricks, *Exit Interviews: Revealing Stories of Why People Are Leaving the Church* (Chicago: Moody, 1993).

[7]Robert E. Webber, *Evangelicals on the Canterbury Trail: Why Evangelicals Are Attracted to the Liturgical Church* (Harrisburg, Pa.: Morehouse, 1985).

changing congregations are fairly obvious. Many are not surprising
and easily explained. Worship styles, attention to children, opportunities for ministry involvement and other assimilation issues
are included in the list of reasons. But the numbers of people
involved in this migration or shopping demand study. The people
who are moving within the church are not unlike the people who
are perhaps watching the church and are moving around it, but
not toward it. They are of the same society and many of its subsets.
An understanding of those who are moving around within the fort
can help us understand those who are still out on the front, and
visa versa.

We turn again to the concept of the mission-sending congregation become a mission outpost, and we can begin to see that the
denominational migration within the church may well be a natural
and needed realignment as the Church positions itself to be more
effective in living the gospel in the midst of and among the surrounding society. Again, the phenomenon is denominational
migration not denominational denial. The author has seen many
Lutherans, Catholics, etc., re-baptized into a Baptist congregation
because of differing denominational understandings of baptism,
and, of course, the migration goes the other way as well. However,
this migration and re-alignment, cannot be expected to happen
without conflict including worship wars. Realignment on a national
denominational level and realignment on a local congregation
doctrinal level are different projects. As was mentioned earlier, the
war that produces sweat in the war rooms of the generals, produces blood on the frontlines of the enlisted personnel. Indeed the
old boot camp saying, "The more you sweat in peace, the less you
bleed in war" is true. There is a need for more sweat in the strategy
planning sessions at the denominational levels (judicatories and
institutions of higher learning); sweat toward attaining peace and
then toward keeping it, and a commitment to the work of "re- (not
de-) denominationalizing" that can make it happen.

At this point it is good for us to revisit Lesslie Newbigin's statement that opens this chapter. He warns us that even "some kind of
federal unity or 'reconciled diversity'" of denominations will be
incapable "of a missionary confrontation with our culture." How
does that relate to our thoughts about "re-denominalization"? My
respect for Lesslie Newbigin's work as missionary, theologian, and
author prevents me from any statement or action that could be
considered a challenge to his observations and interpretations. His
extended time in a markedly different culture than ours can only

close our mouths and open our eyes and ears. It is, in fact, his work that causes me, indeed invites me, to look at our culture and my connection with it and say that a move toward "re-denominalization," this "new order," is not only a step in the direction in which Newbigin is pointing, it is a giant step from what had become traditional denominationalism. I take further comfort in the fact that it is not something that has been manufactured or that I or anyone else am calling for. It is an interpretation of an observation. Denominational migration is the surface evidence of a deeper movement.

The worship that is and isn't happening, and the local, hands-on mission involvement that is or isn't available, the openness to other brothers and sisters in Christ that is or isn't present; realignment is taking place around these points. We must learn why "they" are leaving and why "they" are changing. We must tap into the wisdom and the impulse of the migration. Our investigation into this phenomenon might lead us to questions similar to the questions of those who study migrations in nature. Who teaches the geese and the caribou to migrate, to adjust to their changing environment? Who shows them the way? Could it be the same God, speaking now to the church through his migrating worshipers? We can't go too far with this analogy because geese do not become caribou, even though some Baptists do become Episcopalians, but the point is made with feathers and fur intact. God may be directing us, not to change from something, so much as to adjust our hearts and "family" relationships toward something in response to our environment.

To return to our war analogy, we might ask if the United States military is organized today as it was in World War II. Of course, it isn't. War remains a tragedy. That has not changed. But the tactics of war do change and so, too, the organization and alignment within the military. Like geese and caribou, Marines remain Marines, sailors remain sailors, etc. But the armed forces work together now in ways that would not have been possible years ago. They have adjusted to the changes in the environment of their mission.

New Order Worship

Free-church worship during the final decades of the twentieth century seemed to be reordering itself around two general

approaches: continuing exploration of contemporary possibilities
and a return (the history of Christianity, if not of a particular
denomination, has us use the word "return.") to liturgical patterns.
In the continuing exploration we have seen a path run from
revivalistic, through praise and worship, through seeker, through
gen-X, to alternative. In the return to liturgical patterns we have
seen a path run from revivalistic, through church calendar awareness, to Celtic. No one church or congregation has walked the full
length of or even necessarily far down either path. But the paths
are discernable, with allowances for variations from differing view-
points. These paths do not stop at denominational boundaries
and, in fact, create loosely identified groupings of their own along
the way, bound together, often by worship styles and related
workshops sponsored by a non-denominational organization.
Walkways are paths before they are sidewalks. The people make
paths and eventually those in authority vote to pave some of them.

The decision on the part of a congregation to reorder worship
on a design outside the denomination (Baptists following Pente-
costals) or around a denomination's trends or traditions proved
volatile and contributed to the worship wars. While the option
to reorder worship is most readily observable in the free-church
tradition, it is not confined to non-liturgical settings. A movement
currently gaining momentum within the Roman Catholic church
brings us back to where we started eleven chapters ago. It is
the "Tridentine" movement, motivated by a desire to experience
pre-Vatican II worship. The Tridentine liturgy, technically, "is
the rite codified in the liturgical books promulgated under the
authority of St. Pius V as a response to the wish of the Council of
Trent."[8] However, as one might expect, it is not that simple. Once
an expression of the older generation's protest against the innovations of Vatican II, the movement now includes clergy and laity of
generations of Catholics too young to have experienced the older
liturgy. Once a way of condemning post-Vatican II liturgy, its
emphasis is now "upon defending the values of the Tridentine
mass and its right to exist."[9] This movement parallels the path of
the free-church's return to liturgical patterns mentioned earlier.
The movement has caused Catholics to re-examine what the traditional Roman liturgy actually is. The same thing has happened

---

[8]Laszlo Dobszay, "Ordo Antiquus: The 'Tridentine' Movement and
'Reform of the Reform.'" *Sacred Music* 128:3 (Fall 2001): 14.
[9]Ibid.

within Protestant and free-church traditions. America's worship wars have initiated fresh examinations of what actually lies at the core of worship. The Reformation certainly did not produce one clear, new answer. The question is difficult because Christian worship is dynamic even at its simple core. There, we see that God initiates worship and we respond. It is difficult to keep our response uncluttered and free of attachments. Unfortunately, America's worship wars were/are evidence that people will fight their way back through the attachments on their way to the peace that awaits at the core of worship.

Worship from the Margin

*The cultural war within Christianity
has already ended. Neither side knows it
yet, and neither side can claim victory.
Oh, one side or the other won a small battle
here or there. And a few skirmishes are
still being fought. But, in the end, both
groups will walk away empty-handed.*

Robert N. Nash Jr.[1]

In the so-called liturgical Christian traditions, worship has
always been at the center of congregational life. Only in the last
couple of decades in the U.S. has worship begun to move toward
the center of congregational life in the "free-church" Christian traditions. It is replacing evangelism as the number one Sunday
morning focus of these churches, although in the process of transition, worship and evangelism have overlapped and become entan-
gled. However, while worship has been securing its place in the
center of congregational life in American Christianity, another
movement has also been taking place. American Christianity, both
Catholic and Protestant, has been moving from the core of American society toward the margin. Indeed, all boastings and fanfare of
a Christian "moral majority" were, ironically, cries against a gnaw-
ing awareness of Christianity creeping toward "minority" status.

Vatican II's influence on American Protestantism was the first
evidence that the post-modern movement was underway. Veterans
of the front were quicker to recognize post-modernism. Veterans of

---

[1]*An 8-Track Church in a CD World: The Modern Church in the
Postmodern World* (Macon, Ga.: Smyth & Helwys, 1997), 44. This book is
an excellent and accessible overview of the culture war's (modernity vs.
post-modernity) influence on local congregations.

the fort would speak of the changing face and faith of American society as God bringing the mission field to us; God allowing the United States to be turned into a "foreign" mission field. This could be seen in the people, culture, beliefs, and religions now residing within our borders.

In the modern era, missionaries from the U.S. moved from early methods that "Westernized" the people and Christianity of the foreign countries to allowing, even accommodating, indigenous expressions of the Christian faith. With the foreign mission field moving to America we must re-think what our indigenous culture is. What is the proper indigenous Christian expression of faith in the new mission field called the United States of America?

A "new normalcy"; the thought is chilling. The phrase comes to us from Bob Woodward's *(Washington Post)* interview with Vice President Cheney, published in newspapers across the United States on October 21, 2001. The Vice President was speaking of life in America after September 11, 2001. The new phrase was born of our "new war"; a war that the Vice President said in the same interview, "may never end. At least, not in our lifetime." Throughout the pages of this little book, we have explored the strange phenomenon of a war vocabulary being used to describe developments in Christian worship. The changes have been somewhat painful. At times, it was the pain of loss, at other times, growth pains. During the decades of the 1960s through the end of the century, change was strong and determined, irresistible. It was blessed by some and battled by others, but its presence and power were undeniable.

Were (are) the worship wars "just wars"? In his book *Dispatches From the Front: Theological Engagements with the Secular,* Stanley Hauerwas reminds us that

> A just war is one declared by legitimate authority, whose cause is just, and whose ultimate goal is peace; furthermore, the war must be fought with the right intentions, with a probability for success, with means commensurate to its end, and with a clear respect for non-combatant immunity.[2]

Is any war "just"? While many people say, "Yes," Hauerwas and many others answer with conviction, "No." Are wars inevi-

---

[2]Stanley Hauerwas, *Dispatches From the Front: Theological Engagements with the Secular* (Durham and London: Duke University Press, 1994), 138.

table? Yes. But what is justifiable in the kingdom of this world is not always justifiable within the kingdom of heaven. American Christians are first and foremost, citizens of the kingdom of heaven. Were the worship wars "just?" No. Were the worship wars inevitable? Yes. Worship comes from the heart of people who are agents in the clash between two kingdoms. That was true, even during the era of modernity. It remains true, but compounded, in the transition into the era of post-modernity.

As I write this final segment, the "just-war" theory is receiving fresh attention and America has added two new terms to its sad warfare vocabulary: "new war" and "first war (of the 21st Century)." For Americans, the fort with its vast eastern and western moats has become the front. It is frightening, sad, and life-changing. Yet, like the sun behind a cloud of smoke there is the distinct glimmer of light and hope. Americans have, at least at the time of this writing, risen, if temporarily, to a new level of citizenship that hovers above bipartisanism. One wonders, then, what it will take to bring veterans of the fort and veterans of the front to a worship war bipartisanism. What edifices must crumble? The church will probably not *rise* to a new level of bipartisanism, a revival of patriotism toward the kingdom of heaven. The church will. *lower* itself to this renewed awareness of community and home.

Again, while worship has been moving toward the center of Christianity, Christianity itself has been moving from the center of the American society toward its margin. Christian worship is now and will increasingly become worship from the margin. Worship is different in the church that finds itself out on the edge. In the center of society, the church sat at the head of the banquet table. The popular guest of honor, the church got preferred treatment. No one stepped on its Sunday mornings. Indeed, there was a time in parts of our country during which no one stepped on the church's Wednesday nights. The leaders of worship, when the church was at the center of American society, were honored in their communities as leaders of civic conscience and morality. The church was sought out to give the highest, and often final, word on issues as elections neared. We were a "Christian" nation. In the center of a free and friendly society, the church's worship could expand and breathe deeply the air of the society around it. Worship could reflect the society because, after all, they were we and we were they. Flags in schools and flags in sanctuaries, prayers in sanctuaries and prayers in schools; it was a two-way street right through our neighborhood. We all lived on the same block. Jews? Blacks?

The poor? They had their neighborhoods, their places of worship, and their worship traditions; this was America. Muslims? Buddhists? We sent missionaries to "their" countries. There was no doubt about the identity of the God of our coin inscriptions and pledge of allegiance. It was the God who helped us win all of our wars and who established the seas to protect our eastern and western exposures. Opening prayers and prayer breakfasts in the senates of our states and nation were prayed in Jesus' name. The grand flexibility and openness of our great Christendom were seen in the fact that a Catholic could be elected president of the United States. American Christianity sat on top of all this and its worship continued to reflect its position more and more. Worship could sing society's songs and be shaped by society's values and issues. They were we and we were they. Worship could be evaluated by the American society's understanding of success. Churches could be grown using American business growth strategies. Of course, worship would have to be altered (forgive the misspelled pun) to get the job done, but that was okay because we (the church and society) were all in this together. But then things changed.

After World War II, the ground began to move, but the U.S. was too happy, too prosperous, and too victorious to notice. Society became more open. A nervous eye on the Constitution gave assurance that the openness was American. Everything was, more or less, in place: values (though under some reconsideration after Hiroshima, Nagasaki, and Dresden), patriotism (God still firmly on our side), and the church (agent of our country's righteousness). Worship wobbled a bit, like a tall building in a mild earthquake, but nothing of importance fell off of the altar.

Then came the 1950s: a stalemate in the Korean War and the popularity of Elvis Presley. One had to assume that God had been momentarily distracted. That had to be the case because the Bible says that "He" never sleeps nor slumbers. We were nearly as sure that God, being Christian, was also American. Perhaps Elvis was nothing more than our beloved Bing on steroids, and Korea, we reasoned, wasn't a war after all. Worship, having wobbled, now wavered and wanted to wiggle just a little. Still, God, alone, was worthy of our worship, even though we might have to shore up worship a bit to compensate for this bit of a sag in His Americanism. More patriotism coming in to worship and more evangelism going out of worship might set things back in order. God had let a non-victorious war and rock and roll slip into our country. But, He was still God and a couple of perceived "slip-ups" every two thousand years or so was acceptable. He was still head and shoulders above any other American hero.

Then came the 1960s: Vietnam, Watergate, drugs, civil rights and free love. Where was God? Sing the hymns more loudly. Perhaps he has grown hard of hearing. Sing the hymns more rapidly. Perhaps He is slowing down. Throw the hymns out. Perhaps He has grown bored. We were loosing our grip. Where was God? Our worship was called upon to compensate, to, in fact, hold more tightly to the center.

The following decades saw American society swat the annoying flies of little nuisance wars (little to all except those who fought in them). They weren't big enough to call on God to intervene. Besides, since Korea and Vietnam, He couldn't be counted on as an American warrior anymore. Without war victories to maintain patriotism and, thus, Christianity's American nest, Christianity moved to the right in an attempt to recapture the center for God and country. Worship was "called up" to active duty: catch up with society and bring it back home. We are, after all, one and the same . . . aren't we? . . . weren't we?

Christianity's "slipping" was not about a too lengthy menu of worship styles. From its beginning, Christianity has been more effective in living and communicating its good news when operating at the margin of political power, living among the outsiders. It has been more comfortable in the center, but not more effective. The establishment of our Christian country was the work of "outsiders" who chose the margin to do their work. We owe a great deal to Constantine and his "experiment" that lasted for so long. Be we owe more to the Suffering Servant who, from the margin, dealt with the basics of human existence: water, bread, salt, rest, community, and humility. Out in the margin, the people know about the basics of life, about simplicity, and about the differences between the kingdom of heaven and the kingdom of this world. Political power, privilege, and comfort are confined to the center.

Christian worship in the United States is in transition. The transition was inevitable, has been underway for decades, and is not yet completed. Therefore, we have conflicts among us. Some will fight for the worship we experienced when Christianity was at the center of American society. They continue to pretend that we are in the center or that, at least, a return to the center is within reach. They will fight anything or anyone, even each other, in the fury to recapture the fort. Others know that Christianity now lives in the margins, no matter how much its worship tries to look like the center. The fight seems to be between those who see the ghost of center past and those who see the ghost of center present. Both ghosts scare the margin out of us. Here, in the societal tent city that we once again occupy, Christians, though of a different stripe or style from when we were in the center, are precious and valued brothers and sisters, indeed. Christians who know they are on the margin do not fight and control each other as do those who are trying to hold on to the center. Here we find each other and embrace. Worship from the margin cannot but reflect, now to an extent, eventually more fully, this intensely profound family reunion. Choosing the values and lifestyles of contemporary American society becomes less and less an option for the Christianity that is becoming marginalized, compressed, and, thus, purified.

In 1964 George W. Webber wrote, "Sunday worship by the community was seen as the gathering of Christ's soldiers from their various places of service along the world's battlefronts."[3] He was speaking of worship as preparation for war with the spiritual forces of this world, not *as* war.

What can we do about destructive internal issues and conflicts such as have been experienced in worship? One thing we can do is put our preferred worship style and, indeed, our actual worship experience to the test. Are we worshipping *and* trying to accomplish something else? If so, let's admit that the "something" else is being treated as a god. Christians are to be united by their allegiance to only one God. When that allegiance is divided, the community will be divided.

Another thing we can do is to understand that the Lord does not lead his followers to conflict among themselves. John 17:20–23 was Jesus' prayer for and with his disciples in the upper room not long before he was betrayed and arrested. How can we read this prayer for unity and let "*worship and*" agendas divide us? How can we read this prayer of Jesus and let worship be a point of conflict? Let's bow low before this praying Jesus so that we might rise above the worship of other gods. In worship we are to be focused fully on God the Father, Son, and Holy Spirit. We are to surrender and offer all that we are and all that matters to us to God. Will we hold back just enough to continue the fight; just enough to make sure that there is worship that pleases us?

---

[3] George W. Webber, *The Congregation in Mission: Emerging Structures for the Church in an Urban World* (Nashville: Abingdon, 1964), 106.

Will we hold back enough of our gift to God, enough of our energy and passion to be sure we can suppress any future potential worship war?

Listen again to a portion of Jesus' prayer. The last part of John 17:21 records these words, "so that the world may believe that you have sent me." Evangelism will be the result of brothers and sisters in Christ, worshipping God and nothing or no one else. We must rise to that kind of worship, be led to that kind of community, that kind of family, the kind of unity for which Jesus prayed. It is proper worship from the margin. We spend our lives asking Jesus to answer our prayers. Here is an opportunity for us to answer Jesus' prayer. It begins by having "no other gods" and desiring no other power. It continues by loving God more than worship, by loving our brothers and sisters more than a style. Thomas G. Long encourages us at this point:

> My intuition is that some congregations have managed to avoid the hardened battle lines. . . . What I am referring to, rather, are congregations that have created a new thing in the earth—a service of worship completely attuned to the American cultural moment but also fully congruent with the great worship tradition of the Christian church: a service that attracts young people and seekers and the curious and those who are hungry for a spiritual encounter, but that does so by beckoning people to the deep and refreshing pool of the gospel of Jesus Christ as it has been understood historically in the church.[4]

The worship wars of the mid- to late-twentieth century were inevitable. They were the early evidence that the church was not immune to the culture war between the traditionalists and the progressives. All is not lost, however. It never is for Christians.

There is a way for worship wars to finally cease. There is a way for worship to be the energizing event in Christianity's unifying toward our mission on earth and our home in heaven. It lies in the hope of veterans of the fort and veterans of the front coming to an understanding of the humility of the margin and *the humility of a true worshiper.* There is nothing the bowed creature can do for the enthroned Creator. We cannot impress the Creator. We cannot insist on anything. The humble worshiper is not so presumptuous as to presume or assume. To bow before the throne in our sin,

---

[4] Thomas G. Long, "Between Opposing Forces: Finding a 'Third Way' in Worship," *Congregations* 27:4 (July/August 2001): 8–11.

having nothing to present but the death of God's Son, and to live to tell about it is all grace and gift; God's to us. The humble worshiper knows that worship is not our weekly pat on the back or slap in the face. Either is too self-centered. Humble worship is not morbid. Neither is humble worship the opposite of joyful worship.

Christianity is no longer at the center of American society. Pushed from the center to the outer edge, Christians must see worship and its declaration of our heavenly-kingdom citizenship as a family gathering. In times of crisis, families pull together.

If the veterans of the front used to be the missionaries, and the veterans of the fort were the "church," the time has come for them to combine forces as brothers and sisters in a new normalcy. American Christianity's new normalcy since the beginning of post-modernity is not unlike American society's new normalcy since September 11th. Though it has been in progress since the 1960s, for some, America's post-modern mind-set seems to have arrived almost as suddenly as the terrorist's attack. We have vivid and warm memories of life "before," but we must make adjustments.

Veterans of the fort and veterans of the front, like their "theaters of war," are now mingled together; they are becoming one-and-the-same. They must bow together in the new normalcy's humble worship and then get up off of their knees and together become the new post-modernity's normalcy, the "missional church."[5]

From the margin we will give ourselves to Jesus' agenda rather than asking God to empower and bless ours. We will worship *with* each other instead of *in spite of* or *to spite* each other. Bread and wine will be our banquet. Water will be our sign. God's love for us will be our bond. Jesus will be our model and all we will have to share or fight over will be a portion of the bread, wine, water, and love that Jesus has given us. The power and abundance we have been fighting to retain will have been left back at the center. Shared, simple worship will be the honest expression of a community relegated to the margin. Tents shall be our home. Yet, the gates of hell shall not prevail against the good news born on the margin, returned to the margin, rehearsed through worship, and

---

[5]The important and energizing concept of the "missional church" is put forth in Darrell L. Guder, ed., *Missional Church: A Vision for the Sending of the Church in North America* (Grand Rapids, Mich.: Eerdmans, 1998).

dispersed with cups of water among all those who have also been pushed out to the margin.

> Cure Thy children's warring madness,
> bend our pride to Thy control;
> shame our wanton, selfish gladness,
> rich in things and poor in soul.
> Grant us wisdom, grant us courage,
> Lest we miss Thy kingdom's goal.[6]

Indeed, this is our hope, the fact that people of sound mind and heart detest war, even though it seems we are forced to resort to it from time to time. If that is true of humanity in general, it must surely be intensely true of Christ-followers. War and worship push against each other. Christians are drawn to each other through their kinship in Christ. We must believe and do believe that the worship wars will, one day, end, and that worship will ultimately prevail. It is not necessary, nor is it enough, to relegate that day to the eternal day of heaven. We are drawn together as we are drawn toward God in worship. It can and must happen "on earth, as it is in heaven."

What will worship's music be on that day? It will be a music refined by the fire of worship wars, tempered by the twin passions of worship and sharing the gospel. Our desire to reform worship without rejecting it will lead us to music that lifts us from the futility and self-centeredness of fighting each other to the unity of work and worship that Jesus himself prayed for in John 17. I believe the music on that day will support cross-generational worship.

Our hymnals are bound evidence that peace can prevail in worship. They are ecumenical, no matter their title, and contain a variety of musical styles. The music projected on our screens represents worship that lifts our vision beyond our differences, beyond us. Can worship be redeemed and its wars brought to peace by simply paying attention to the texts of its repertory? I hold out this hope and present its challenge. The power of music that has been allowed to contribute to worship's wars can, and must, be put to the task of helping to facilitate worship's peace.

---

[6]Harry Emerson Fosdick, "God of Grace and God of Glory," 1930 (copyright Elinor Fosdick) in *The Hymnal 1982: According to the Use of the Episcopal Church* (New York: Church Hymnal Corp., 1985).

Bibliography

Books

Barna, George. *The Frog in the Kettle: What Christians Need to Know About Life in the 21st Century*. Ventura, Calif.: Regal Books, 1990.

Best, Harold M. *Music Through The Eyes of Faith*. San Francisco: Harper, 1993.

Bruce, Steve. *Pray TV: Televangelism in America*. New York: Rutledge, Chapman, & Hall, 1990.

Bruggemann, Walter. *Israel's Praise: Doxology Against Idolatry and Ideology*. Philadelphia: Fortress, 1988.

Callahan, Kennon L. *Effective Church Leadership*. San Francisco: Harper, 1990.

Cantor, Norman F. *The Age of Protest: Dissent and Rebellion in the Twentieth Century*. New York: Hawthorn Books, 1969.

Clark, M. Edward, et al., eds. *The Church Creative: A Reader on the Renewal of the Church*. Nashville: Abingdon, 1967.

Corbitt, J. Nathan. *The Sound of the Harvest: Music's Mission in Church and Culture*. Grand Rapids: Baker, 1998.

Dawn, Marva J. *Reaching Out Without Dumbing Down* Grand Rapids: Eerdmans, 1995.

Dockery, David S., ed. *New Dimensions in Evangelical Thought: Essays in Honor of Millard J. Erickson*. Downers Grove, Ill.: InterVarsity, 1998.

Doran, Carol, and Thomas H. Troeger. *Trouble at the Table: Gathering the Tribes for Worship*. Nashville: Abingdon, 1992.

Duck, Ruth C. *Finding Words for Worship: A Guide for Leaders*. Louisville: Westminster John Knox, 1995.

Duke, David Nelson, and Paul D. Duke. *Anguish and the Word: Preaching That Touches Pain*. Macon, Ga.: Smyth & Helwys, 1992.

Flannery, Austin, O.P., ed. *Vatican Council II: Constitutions, Decrees, Declarations.* Northport, N.Y.: Costello Publishing Company, 1996.

Fox, Matthew. *On Becoming a Musical, Mystical Bear.* New York: Paulist, 1976.

Frank, Thomas Edward. *The Soul of the Congregation: An Invitation to Congregational Reflection.* Nashville: Abingdon, 2000.

Goethals, Gregor T. *The TV Ritual: Worship at the Video Altar.* Boston: Beacon, 1981.

Good News for Modern Man: The New Testament in Today's English Version. American Bible Society, 1966.

Graham, Billy. *The Jesus Generation.* Minneapolis: World Wide Publications, 1971.

Guder, Darrell L., ed. *Missional Church: A Vision for the Sending of the Church in North America.* Grand Rapids: Eerdmans, 1998.

Guinness, Os. *Dining with the Devil: The Megachurch Movement Flirts with Modernity.* Grand Rapids: Baker, 1993.

Hendricks, William D. *Exit Interviews: Revealing Stories of Why People are Leaving the Church.* Chicago: Moody, 1993.

Hesselbein, Frances, et al., eds. *The Community of the Future.* San Francisco: Jossey-Bass, 1998.

Hill, Brennen R. *Exploring Catholic Theology: God, Jesus, Church and Sacraments.* Mystic, Conn.: Twenty-Third Publications, 1995.

Hunter, James Davison. *Culture Wars: The Struggle to Define America.* New York: Basic Books, 1991.

Hustad, Donald P. *Jubilate! Church Music in the Evangelical Tradition.* Carol Stream, Ill.: Hope Publishing Company, 1981.

———. *Jubilate II: Church Music in Worship and Renewal.* Carol Stream, Ill.: Hope Publishing Company, 1993.

Jones, Cheslyn, et al. *The Study of Liturgy.* Rev. ed. New York: Oxford University Press, 1992.

Kierkegaard, Søren. *Purity of Heart Is to Will One Thing.* New York: Harper, 1938.

L'Engle, Madeleine. *Walking on Water: Reflections on Faith and Art.* Wheaton, Ill.: Harold Shaw Publishers, 1980.

Lee, Robert, ed. *Cities and Churches: Readings on the Urban Church.* Philadelphia: Westminster, 1962.

The Living Bible: Paraphrased. Wheaton, Ill.: Tyndale, 1971.

Living Letters. Wheaton, Ill.: Tyndale, 1962.

Marty, Martin E. *Pilgrims in Their Own Land: 500 Years of Religion in America.* New York: Penguin, 1984.

Morgenthaler, Sally. *Worship Evangelism*. Grand Rapids: Zondervan, 1995.

Nash, Robert N., Jr. *An 8–Track Church in a CD World: The Modern Church in the Postmodern World*. Macon, Ga.: Smyth & Helwys, 1997.

Newbigin, Lesslie. *Foolishness to the Greeks: The Gospel and Western Culture*. Grand Rapids: Eerdmans, 1987.

Noble, David F. *The Religion of Technology: The Divinity of Man and the Spirit of Invention*. New York: Knopf, 1997.

Palmer, Parker J. *To Know As We Are Known: Education as a Spiritual Journey*. San Francisco: Harper, 1983.

Peacock, Charlie. *At the Cross Roads: An Insider's Look at the Past, Present, and Future of Contemporary Christian Music*. Nashville: Broadman & Holman, 1999.

Peterson, John W. *The Miracle Goes On: An Autobiography*. Grand Rapids: Zondervan, 1976.

Ramshaw, Gail. *God Beyond Gender: Feminist Christian God-Language*. Minneapolis: Fortress, 1995.

Reich, Charles A. *The Greening of America*. New York: Random House, 1970.

Roszak, Theodore. *The Making of a Counter Culture: Reflections on the Technocratic Society and Its Youthful Opposition*. Garden City, N.Y.: Doubleday, 1968.

Schultze, Quentin J. *Televangelism and American Culture: The Business of Popular Religion*. Grand Rapids: Baker, 1991.

Senter, Mark, III. *The Coming Revolution in Youth Ministry*. Wheaton, Ill.: Victor, 1992.

Streiker, Lowell D. *The Jesus Trip: Advent of the Jesus Freaks*. Nashville: Abingdon, 1971.

Stringfellow, William. *Dissenter in a Great Society: A Christian View of America in Crisis*. New York: Holt, Rinehart & Winston, 1966.

Wagner, C. Peter. *Your Church Can Grow: Seven Vital Signs of a Healthy Church*. Ventura, Calif.: Regal, 1976.

Webber, George W. *The Congregation in Mission*. Nashville: Abingdon, 1964.

Webber, Robert E. *Evangelicals on the Canterbury Trail: Why Evangelicals Are Attracted to the Liturgical Church*. Harrisburg, Pa.: Morehouse, 1985.

―――. *Signs of Wonder: The Phenomenon of Convergence in Modern Liturgical and Charismatic Churches*. Nashville: Abbott Martyn, 1992.

————. *Worship Is a Verb: Eight Principles for Transforming Worship.* 2d ed. Peabody, Mass.: Hendrickson, 1992.

Webster, Douglas D. *Selling Jesus: What's Wrong with Marketing the Church.* Downers Grove, Ill.: InterVarsity, 1992.

Wind, James P., and James W. Lewis. *American Congregations, Volume 1: Portraits of Twelve Religious Communities.* Chicago: University of Chicago Press, 1994.

Wren, Brian. *What Language Shall I Borrow? God-Talk in Worship: A Male Response to Feminist Theology.* New York: Crossroad, 1995.

Wuthnow, Robert. *The Restructuring of American Religion: Society and Faith Since World War II.* Princeton, N.J.: Princeton University Press, 1988.

Young, Carlton R., ed. *Duty and Delight: Routley Remembered, A Memorial Tribute to Erik Routley (1917–1982).* Carol Stream, Ill.: Hope Publishing Company, 1985.

Hymnals, Song Collections, and Musicals

Batastini, Robert J., ed. *Worship: A Hymnal and Service Book for Roman Catholics.* 3d ed. Chicago: GIA Publications, 1986.

Bock, Fred., ed. *Hymns for the Family of God.* Nashville: Paragon Associates, 1976.

————, ed. *Worship His Majesty.* Alexandria, Ind.: Gaither Music Company, 1987.

Brink, Emily R., ed. *Psalter Hymnal.* Grand Rapids: CRC Publications, 1987.

Carmichael, Ralph, and Kurt Kaiser. *Tell It Like It Is: A Folk Musical for Choir and Solos.* Waco, Tex.: Lexicon Music, 1969.

Carmichael, Ralph, et al. *The New Church Hymnal.* Lexicon Music, 1976.

Glover, Raymond F., et al. *The Hymnal 1982: According to the Use of The Episcopal Church.* New York: Church Publishing Incorporated, 1985.

Hustad, Donald P., ed. *Hymns for the Living Church.* Carol Stream, Ill.: Hope Publishing Company, 1974.

————. *The Singing Church.* Carol Stream, Ill.: Hope Publishing Company, 1985.

Kendrick, Graham. *The Collection.* Great Britain: Kingsway Music, 1992.

Lutheran Book of Worship. Minneapolis: Augsburg Publishing House and Philadelphia: Board of Publication, Lutheran Church in America, 1978.

McKinney, B. B., ed. *The Broadman Hymnal*. Nashville: Broadman, 1940.

Oldenburg, Bob. *Good News: A Christian Folk-Musical*. Nashville: Broadman, 1967.

Reynolds, William J., ed. *Baptist Hymnal* (1975 Edition). Nashville: Convention Press, 1975.

Service Book and Hymnal. Minneapolis: Augsburg Publishing House and Philadelphia: Lutheran Church in America, 1958.

Sims, W. Hines, ed. *Baptist Hymnal*. Nashville: Convention Press, 1956.

Young, Carlton R., ed. *The United Methodist Hymnal: Book of United Methodist Worship*. Nashville: United Methodist Publishing House, 1989.

Periodical Literature

Bierly, Steve. "Sparring Over Worship." *Leadership* (Winter 1997): 37–39.

Burge, Gary M. "Missing God at Church?" *Christianity Today* (October 6, 1997): 22, 27.

Burghardt, Walter J. "Just Word and Just Worship: Biblical Justice and Christian Liturgy." *Worship* 73:5 (September, 1999).

Crabtree, Cameron. "Music Exec Notes: Impact on Contemporary Music." *Gate Way: Golden Gate Baptist Theological Seminary Magazine for Alumni and Friends* (Spring 2001): 7.

Dart, John. "Church Shoppers—Many Newcomers in the Pews." *Christian Century* (January 30–February 6, 2002).

Davis, Vernon. "The Unsettled Landscape of Theological Education." *Review & Expositor* 95:4 (Fall 1998): 485–90.

Dobszay, Laszlo. "Ordo Antiquus: The 'Tridentine' Movement and 'Reform of the Reform.'" *Sacred Music* 128:3 (Fall 2001).

Dulles, Avery. "The Ways We Worship." *First Things* (March 1998): 28.

Forbis, Wesley L. "Currents and Cross Currents Impacting Hymnal Formation: The New Baptist Hymnal, Issues and Answers." *Review & Expositor* 87:1 (Winter 1990): 75–88.

Gold, Todd. "Amy Grant: Music From the Heart." *Saturday Evening Post* (May/June 1986): 43–45.

Keller, Catherine. "Inventing the Goddess: A Study in Ecclesial Backlash." *Christian Century* (April 6, 1994): 340–42.

Knox, Marv. "Call a Truce to Music Wars." *Church Musician Today* 4:6 (February 2001): 21.

Long, Thomas G. "Between Opposing Forces: Finding a 'Third Way' in Worship." *Congregations* 27:4 (July/August 2001): 8–11.

Marty, Martin E. "Reflections on Graham by a Former Grump." *Christianity Today* 32:17 (November 18, 1988): 24–25.

Pennington-Russell, Julie. "From Your Pastor." *The Calvary Tower* [congregational newsletter of Calvary Baptist Church, Waco, Tex.] 33:44 (November 4, 1998).

Peters, Ted. "Worship Wars." *Dialog* 33:3 (Summer 1999): 166–72.

Phan, Peter C. "How Much Uniformity Can We Stand? How Much Unity Do We Want? Church and Worship in the Next Millennium." *Worship* (May 1998): 194–210.

Rathke, Michael. "An Apology for the Preservation of Archaic Language in Hymnody." *American Organist* 35:9 (September 2001).

Rausch, Thomas P., S.J. "The Unfinished Agenda of Vatican II." *America* (June 17, 1995): 23–27.

Small, Joseph D. and Burgess, John P. "Evaluating 'Re-Imagining': Reformed and Reformulating." *Christian Century* (April 6, 1994): 342ff.

Trueheart, Charles. "Welcome to the Next Church." *Atlantic Monthly* (August 1996): 37–58.

Walsh, Christopher, J. "Minding Our Language: Issues of Liturgical Language Arising in Revision." *Worship* 74:6 (November 2000): 482–503.

Unpublished Materials

Forbis, Wesley L. "Position Statement." Manual: Hymnal Committees. Church Music Department, Baptist Sunday School Board, Southern Baptist Convention, 1987.

Index